D0840139

THE
LIVE | DEⱯD JOURNAL

30 DAYS OF PRAYER FOR UNREACHED PEOPLES

Copyright © 2012 AGWM Africa
ALL RIGHTS RESERVED.

Published by Abide Publishers LLC
1600 N. Boonville, Suite B&C, Springfield, MO 65803

Cover design, typesetting, and interior design by Lucent Digital
www.lucentdigital.co

No portion of this book may be reproduced, stored in a retrieval
system, or transmitted in any form or by any means—electronic,
mechanical, photocopy, recording, or any other—except for brief
quotations in printed reviews, without the prior written permission
of the publisher.

ISBN 978-0-9981789-8-1

Printed in the United States of America

take the whole Gospel to
the whole world

LIVE | DEAD   EAST AFRICA

This journal is dedicated to the unreached by the contributing writers from around the world. As one small part of the body of Christ, we are thrilled to align ourselves with all who live and die for God's glory among all peoples.

May the whole church indeed take the whole gospel to the whole world. And may the unreached of East Africa represented in this journal be among the first to experience the joy of salvation.

War.

Growth.

And people who do not know the Lord ask why in the world we waste our lives as missionaries. They forget that they too are expending their lives and when the bubble has burst they will have nothing of eternal significance to show for the years they have wasted.   – NATE SAINT, MARTYR

TABLE OF CONTENTS

Spirit.

6	Introduction to Living Dead
16	Day 1: Abide
20	Day 2: Lost
24	Day 3: Simplicity
28	Day 4: Sacrifice
34	Day 5: Spiritual Warfare
38	Day 6: Expectations
42	Day 7: Integrity in Speech
46	Day 8: Passion
52	Day 9: Persecution
56	Day 10: Abandon
60	Day 11: Prophecy
64	Day 12: Transparency
72	Day 13: Affirmation
76	Day 14: A Learning Heart
80	Day 15, Part 1: Servanthood
84	Day 15, Part 2: Three Martyrdoms
90	Day 16: Mobility
96	Day 17: Scriptures
100	Day 18: Apostolic Function
104	Day 19: Proclamation
108	Day 20: Suffering
116	Day 21: Worship
120	Day 22: Flexibility
124	Day 23: Hospitality
128	Day 24: Giving
136	Day 25: Humility
140	Day 26: Followership
144	Day 27: Team
148	Day 28: Pioneering
154	Day 29: Forgiveness
158	Day 30: Pentecost
162	Final Thoughts
166	About the Collaborators

HOW TO LIVE DEAD

If you've accepted Jesus as your Savior, living dead in Christ is not a mere concept. It is an indisputable fact. Romans 6:1-11 makes it clear that through the death of our Savior, we also have the opportunity to die to self, living in and through Him. Our sins have been cleared out and replaced with His Spirit. We are put into Him. Thankfully, living in Christ is not about our striving. All we must do to "live dead" is simply *trust His Spirit to do in us what we cannot do in ourselves.*

You may read the title of this journal and think, *I can't live dead. It's just too hard. I slip up so often!* Guess what: We all do! But if you have accepted Christ, you are dead already. You must, however, learn to *remain dead.* The secret to remaining dead is the joy of abiding. In abiding, we find God's will and He enables us to exchange our desires for His master plan. In abiding, somehow things such as our comfort, timelines, preferences, and control seem insignificant in comparison to His glory.

As you abide in Christ, listen to His heart. It beats for lost people. Just as He died for the lost, He asks that we also die to our selfish ambitions and, with reckless abandon, share Him. Our Savior asks that we go to all who are lost.

In this journal, however, *we ask that you consider those who are not just lost, but those who are also unreached and unengaged.* You will be praying daily for people who have no Bible in their language, no church, no missionaries, no believers, and no access to Jesus. They are inconvenient to reach. It takes blood, sweat, and tears to show them the love of Jesus. Only those who have learned to live dead will reach them.

Jesus told us that "the seed that falls to the ground and dies produces many seeds." As you work through this journal, present yourself to God as that dead seed. And as your character is conformed to Christ's, may your first prayer be, "God, how would you like for me to respond to the unreached and unengaged?"

We trust that He will answer your prayer and that your 30-day prayer journey will be an adventuresome one—alive in Him.

HOW TO USE THIS JOURNAL

This journal is designed to be a 30-day prayer journey. Each day will include information on an unreached people group and a reflection on what it means to live dead. You will also have space to respond to the readings, answer some challenge questions, and write a prayer. Each day will present a challenge, a practical way that you can live dead. Each chapter is written by a missionary or a mission-hearted person who has committed to live dead.

There are different ways to use the journal, but I suggest it will be most rewarding if you do the following:

- Read only one chapter a day. Use the journal as a supplement to your Bible reading time.
- Pray over the people group mentioned in that chapter.
- Pray that Jesus would send missionaries to them.
- Pray that the Scripture would be made available in their language.
- Pray that influential men and women from that people would be saved.
- Ask Jesus if He wants you to go—to live and die among that people.
- Record your thoughts, reflections, and prayers in the journal space provided. If you don't know what to write, just write out a prayer for the people group that you read about that day or write out a prayer for help in responding to the "Live Dead Challenge" presented in that chapter, or do both.
- Work through the journal as a family or a group of friends. Keep each other accountable to the challenges.

Prayer should never be
understood primarily in terms of
power but rather as relating to
God who is the source of all power.

– DR. GAILYN VAN RHEENEN, DIRECTOR OF MISSION ALIVE

HOW TO PRAY FOR UNREACHED PEOPLE GROUPS

Each chapter of the *Live Dead Journal* ends with information on an unreached people group in East Africa and suggests a creative reminder for prayer. If you have never prayed for an unreached people group, here are some helpful kingdom prayers:

1 | PRAY THAT THE WORD OF GOD WOULD RISE.

There is no substitute for the Word of God. Pray for the Bible to be translated into their language. Pray for the "Jesus" film to be made available in their language. Pray for the dissemination of the Word in printed, audio, and video formats. Pray that every member of that people group would be exposed to Scripture.

2 | PRAY THAT THE LORD OF THE HARVEST WOULD SEND FORTH LABORERS INTO THE HARVEST FIELD.

The entire Live Dead strategy is based on teams living and dying among God's precious lost ones. Pray that Jesus would send missionaries from your church to the people group; pray for multinational teams to be formed; pray for near-culture neighbors to be gripped with the lostness of the people next to them.

3 | PRAY THAT THE SPIRIT OF GOD, THE HOLY SPIRIT, WILL BE POURED OUT ON ALL FLESH.

This promise is also for "… all those who are far off." Pray that various members of the unreached people group will be filled and empowered by the Holy Spirit. Pray for men and women, young and old, poor and rich, marginalized and influential. Pray for a mighty filling of the Holy Spirit for those who come to Christ, that they might have power and passion to reach others in their tribe, and to attack evil wherever they find it.

4 | PRAY THAT THE CROSS WILL BE UNVEILED.

Many of the people groups you will be praying for are Muslim. Muslims especially, but all peoples, have been blinded by the devil. They misunderstand or reject the atoning work of Christ on the cross. Pray that their eyes will be opened to the blessed irrationality of a God becoming man, and then dying a shameful death for our redemption.

5 | PRAY THAT THE HOLY SPIRIT WOULD UNITE THE BODY OF CHRIST.

None of us lives or works in a vacuum. Pray for the first believers in the people group. Pray that there would be loving, trusting communion between them. Pray against jealousies and the lies of the devil. Pray for the missionaries working among those people. Pray for unity, blessing, and joy in the Holy Spirit. Division among new believers and missionary colleagues is a primary tool of the devil. Pray for God's blessed unity to prevail.

6 | PRAY FOR MEN AND WOMEN OF PEACE.

Often a key person opens the way for a whole people to receive Christ. Sometimes this person of peace accepts the Lord and leads others to Christ; at other times this person grants permission for ministry in a certain area even if he does not convert himself. Pray that men and women of influence would come to Jesus from each people group and lead their people to faith in Christ. Pray for the emergence of house churches that reproduce, and elders that rise up to lead the new movement.

HOW TO ABIDE IN JESUS

The first chapter of this journal is foundational to the whole Live Dead concept. The chapter is on abiding in Christ, which essentially means we spend extravagant time with Jesus on a daily basis. From that abiding time will come the strength and direction to fulfill the Live Dead challenge. As you read the first chapter, you may be surprised to find that I call you to give Jesus a tithe of your day for a month. That means two and a half hours a day! For all of us, this seems like an impossible challenge. It is not impossible. It is difficult, to be sure, but who said dying is easy? It can be done, if you want it badly enough.

I don't usually invest a full two and a half hours every day. Most days it is closer to an hour and a half or two hours. The point is not legalism, for legalism spoils everything. The point is valuing Jesus so highly that we give Him extravagant daily time and we long to be with Him as much as we can.

Here is what I do and about how long it takes me (this can be done early in the morning, late at night, or even split up through the day: an hour in the morning, a half hour prayer at lunch time, an hour in the evening, etc.):

READ THE BIBLE | ONE HOUR

- Three Old Testament chapters, one Psalm, one chapter from the Gospels, one chapter from Acts or the epistles.
- I read sequentially. So if today I read Joshua 1, 2, and 3; Psalm 1; Matthew 1; and Romans 1, then tomorrow would be Joshua 4, 5, and 6; Psalm 2; Matthew 2; and Romans 2.
- I underline in my Bible and make small notes. I summarize each chapter with a phrase that I write in my Bible at the top of the page. I draw small pictures and connect similar thoughts with lines across the page, circle parallel language, put in exclamation points, stars and happy and sad faces—my Bible looks scribbled in, but it helps me process what I am reading.
- I pull out one key verse or thought from each section of reading and enter it into my journal. I then look at the summaries in my journal and write half a journal page in response to what I have read.

- If I come across a verse that reminds me of a song, I stop and sing the song.
- If I come across a prayer, I stop and personalize the prayer.
- If I come across a challenging thought, I stop and meditate on it for a while.

MEMORIZE SCRIPTURE | FIVE MINUTES

I try to memorize about three verses a week. Every day I will spend a few minutes reviewing them and adding another verse. When a new week rolls around, I pick three different verses. I don't worry about retaining the previous week's verses but do try to keep the current week's verses in mind all week long.

Memorizing Scripture is my first defense against errant and impure thoughts. When the wrong thoughts come, it does not help me to try not to think them (ironically, that often just reinforces them); rather, I begin to quote out loud the Scripture I have been working on that week. I bump out the errant thoughts with God's thoughts. It is a wonderful help toward pure thinking.

PRAY | 30 MINUTES

I have a prayer list that includes family, friends, colleagues, unsaved neighbors, leaders, and unreached peoples. I pray through it every day.

I pray in the Spirit. Because my mind wanders so easily, I like to combine my prayer time with exercise. I will run out a distance from my house until I have had a good workout, and then walk back. As I walk, I pray. Sometimes I will pick an object in the far distance and pray in the Spirit until I have walked past that object. This helps discipline me to pray with my spirit as well as with my mind (1 Corinthians 14:15).

Sometimes I work through the simple acrostic ACTS: adoration, confession, thanksgiving, supplication.

WORSHIP | 30 MINUTES

I love old hymns. I will sit at the piano and bang out hymns and sing and worship Jesus. You may play an instrument or you may enjoy listening to music on your iPod. It doesn't matter. Lift your voice and sing to Jesus.

Remember that worship is more than singing. I love to praise the Lord. I tell Him in my own words, out loud, why and how much I love Him. I declare His praises, proclaim His nature. I remind myself and the powers that be that God is good and His mercy endures forever.

LISTENING | FIVE TO 10 MINUTES

I find it helpful to take at least five minutes at the end of my abiding time and just linger in the sweet presence of Jesus. I try to quiet my mind, emptying it of all my thoughts and just wait on the Lord. I try to listen for His still small voice. Is there anything He wants to whisper to me? It is a great way to end the time of abiding.

Sometimes I start my abiding time this way, and a good cup of chai seems to clear the heavens for me.

AN ENCOURAGEMENT TO MOMS AND OTHER SAINTS

Life sometimes dictates to us how we spend our time. Not everyone has the luxury of multiple free hours in a row to spend alone with God. Parents of small children barely have time to breathe, let alone contemplate the heaven of two hours of stillness. Jesus understands where you are and loves you for it. I am sure the Lord is not offended at our multi-tasking. Pray when you wash the dishes, worship on your morning jog, pray with your spouse walking the dog in the park, sing in the spirit whenever you drive. We strive for extended periods alone with Jesus, but sometimes the stage of life we are in demands time to be offered in multiple little chunks while we stand, run, walk, drive, or rock a baby to sleep.

There is no prescribed way to spend extravagant time with Jesus. The Bible and prayer are, of course, the foundations, but in those and from those there is much variety. God made you unique, and your rhythm and season of life will likely be much different from mine. The point is to enjoy Jesus and to give Him extravagant daily time. However that works best for you … go for it!

To live dead is as much about living for and with Jesus as it is about dying to self. Thus the Live Dead challenge centers on Jesus. Jesus is our everything. Giving Jesus extravagant daily time will "life" you. His life in you will give you the courage and desire to die to self. The result will not only be inward joy, it will also be outward blessing—even to the uttermost parts and unreached peoples of the earth.

—DICK BROGDEN

A PLACE STAMP HERE NO POSTAGE NECESSARY IF MAILED IN THE UNITED STATES

I used to think that prayer should have the first place and teaching the second.

I now feel it would be truer to give prayer the first, second and third places and teaching the fourth.

– JAMES O. FRASER

ABIDING: EXTRAVAGANT TIME WITH JESUS
BY DICK BROGDEN | SUDAN

"Abide in me, and I in you. As the branch cannot bear fruit of itself, unless it abides in the vine, neither can you, unless you abide in me. I am the vine, you are the branches. He who abides in me, and I in him, bears much fruit; for without me you can do nothing. ... You did not choose me, but I chose you and appointed you that you should go and bear fruit, and that your fruit should remain, that whatever you ask the Father in my name he may give you."

JOHN 15:4-5, 16

Jesus is our priceless treasure. Because Jesus is worthy, because Jesus is worth it, "the whole church must take the whole gospel to the whole world" (Lausanne Covenant, 1974). As we fall deeper in love with Jesus, we become like Him. To be like Jesus is to love the nations of the world. To love the nations is to proclaim to them the gospel. The gospel is what God has done for us in Christ.

I am not the gospel. You are not the gospel. What you and I do is not the gospel. The gospel applies to all people everywhere, across all ages and cultures. The gospel is what God has done, is doing, and will do in Christ. A Christ-centered gospel demands therefore a Christ-centered missionary. If we are to be faithful in proclaiming Christ, we must know Him intimately.

We can only know Jesus intimately if we spend extravagant daily time with Him. Extravagant time with Jesus on a daily basis is the foundation of all fruitfulness. This is true biblically, historically, and experientially. Jesus spent close to 90 percent of his life in a village of 12 families, and even His three years of ministry were marked by time alone with the Father. Moses spent 40 years in Midian and had multiple trips to the mountain with God. Paul spent 13 years in preparation, some or much of it in the Arabian Desert, and prayed constantly. Adam, Joseph, David, Elijah, Daniel, Mary, John, and others all gave God extravagant time.

There is no hero of the faith who did not linger daily with Jesus. In *Heroes*, Harold Sala tells the story of David Livingstone, who faced great loneliness in Africa after his wife, Mary, died. After 16 years in Africa he returned to give a lecture at the University of Glasgow. One of his arms was useless as a result of a lion attack, and his body was wasted from 27 bouts with malaria. His face was full of wrinkles from the wear and tear of daily living. A hush crept over the students as he spoke: "Shall I tell you what sustained me amidst the trials and hardships and loneliness of my exiled life? ... It was a promise, the promise of a gentleman of the most sacred honor; it was this promise, 'Lo, I am with you always, even unto the end of the world.' " At Livingstone's death, his body was found bent in prayer, kneeling at his bed. His Bible was open to Matthew 28. In the margin was a small notation: "The word of a Gentleman."

John York, humble missionary to Africa, was no stranger to pressure and suffering, dying too young from leukemia. He said, "There is no 'Go' without 'Lo.' " First we are called to Jesus; He is with us always, and we with Him. Then we go ... to the uttermost parts and pressures of the earth.

God has all resources. As we abide in Jesus, He pours Himself into us. When we are full of Jesus—His Spirit, His love—this fullness affects our spirits, it "lifes" us, it keeps us sweet and simple. From there we bless others near us; from there we bless the world. The abiding value simply means we take extravagant time with Jesus daily. While we will all do this differently, the essentials are time in God's Word, the Bible, and in God's presence, prayer. The specifics are up to you. There will be many variables. There will be seasons of life. But together we declare that above all else we value Jesus. His person, His presence is everything to us, and we will demonstrate this by giving Him extravagant time daily.

LIVE DEAD CHALLENGE

We all understand the principle of the financial tithe. All our resources belong to God, and we merely return (at a minimum) 10 percent of what is already His and He takes the balance and blesses it to meet our needs.

I suggest that the same principle applies to our time. If we will tithe back to Jesus 10 percent of the time He has given us, He will take what remains of the day and bless it, making it more fruitful than we can believe possible.

A tithe of a day is roughly two and a half hours. *The Live Dead challenge is to tithe your time to Jesus every day for the next month. Give Jesus two and a half hours a day—or as close to it as you possibly can.* (An example of how to do this is included in the introduction.) Die to your own schedule, go to bed earlier, get up earlier, give up TV, do whatever you have to do to make it possible to spend extravagant daily time with Jesus.

Give Jesus extravagant time today. Commit to giving him extravagant time every day for the next 30 days, no matter what you have to drop in order to make it happen.

UNREACHED PEOPLE GROUP

RASHAIDA

The Rashaida are known as a fierce warrior people group. However, if you show up at their tent uninvited, they will ask you in for a cup of tea and coffee. Their lives are built around Muslim traditions that have lasted for centuries. These traditions include big families, hospitality, praying regularly to Allah, hard work, and sacrifice. The men are famous for sword dancing and the women for beadwork, which can be seen on front of their burqas.

They are a desert people group of more than 100,000 people. We do not know of one who believes in Jesus as his Savior.

Pray for Rashaida people today every time you see a Toyota. The Bedouin Rashaida cherish their Toyotas almost as much as their camels—they are often used for smuggling goods across the desert. Rashaida boys learn to drive them at about 10 years old.

Today, my response to tithing my time is:

LOST: PARABLE OF THE FATHER'S HEART
BY ELI GAUTREAUX | TEXAS

"For the Son of Man came to seek and save what was lost."

Luke 19:10

Several years ago, my family and I attended a conference on a university campus. One afternoon our 4-year-old went missing from the student center where I had been working. As it became apparent that my little girl was lost, my heart sank, and with each passing moment I began to feel more and more nauseous. Words cannot describe the depth of anguish and despair I felt that day. With the help of university police, we frantically searched all four floors of that building, eventually spilling out into the parking lot and covering the four city blocks of the campus. She was completely lost.

In Luke 15, we read Jesus' three parables about lost things—the lost sheep, the lost coin, and the lost sons. Contextually, however, the emphases lay not on the things lost, but rather on those to whom the lost things belonged—the shepherd, the woman, the father. The third parable is frequently called the Parable of the Prodigal Son—but as G. Campbell Morgan suggested, perhaps a better name would be the title he chose for his book, *The Parable of the Father's Heart,* for in this story we see the broken heart of God revealed. This father was actively watching, waiting, and yearning to be reunited with his lost child. That is exactly the way God feels about every one of His children who are lost and separated from Him.

Morgan wrote in *The Great Physician:* "It is well now to remind ourselves that when we speak of a lost man or woman, the final emphasis in our thinking should not be on the lost person, but on the one who has lost that person. When we speak of a man being lost, do we think most about his suffering, or of the suffering of God?" When the devil has kidnapped a child of God, it is God who hurts the deepest, who suffers most. His heart is broken as He can foresee the inevitable consequence of lost relationship—eternal separation. When I remember the way I felt about my one lost child, I cannot begin to imagine the Father's exponential pain over the multitude of His lost children from every corner of the earth. When my daughter was lost, I wanted everyone everywhere to drop what they were doing and help me find her. It was inconceivable to me that anyone, especially those I loved most, would be able to rest until she was safely found.

In 2 Samuel 23, we read about three of David's mighty men who heard a sigh from their king's lips—his simple longing for a drink of water from the well near the gate at Bethlehem. Risking their own lives, they crossed enemy lines in the dark of night and retrieved the drink of water for their king. It is clear that these three men were close enough to their king, in proximity but more importantly in relational intimacy, to hear the longing of his heart. They were never given a command. Their king's longing became their immediate, voluntary, and dangerous mission.

After the longest hour of my life—in which every passing minute felt like an eternity—we found our daughter. The moment I saw her, I had an instant understanding of the joy in heaven that erupts when a lost person is reunited with the Father. I cried out with happiness and could not stop hugging her. The intensity of the darkness that had accompanied her loss was matched only by the elation I felt when I held her in my arms again.

LIVE DEAD CHALLENGE

Today as you pray, rather than pouring out *your* heart to God, ask Him to pour *His* heart to you. Our King is a wonderful and loving Father who suffers deeply at the loss of His children. If we love Him, we will listen. Eventually we will feel His broken heart. If we love Him we will, like the mighty men of old, make His longing our mission no matter what the risk. What is the cry of God's heart? He is weeping over His lost children, watching, waiting, and yearning for them to come home.

TIGRE

The Tigre are Muslim
nomadic people who inhabit
the northern, western, and
coastal lowlands of Eritrea as
well as areas in eastern Sudan.
Most of them belong to Sunni Islam.

The Tigre suffered persecution from the Marxist
government of Ethiopia in the 1970s and 1980s, since they
were both nomadic and Muslim. The government's efforts to
settle the Tigre, combined with the Eritrean–Ethiopian War,
resulted in the resettling of tens of thousands of Tigre in
Sudan. Half of the Tigre live among the Beni-Amer as serfs
and workers.

**Every time you see a symbol of restricted freedom,
a jail, a chain, handcuffs, or read about slavery, pray
for a people—now serfs to both Islam and other
tribes—that they may become sons and daughters of
the Heavenly Father.**

Life is pitiful, death so familiar, suffering and pain so common, yet I would not be anywhere else. Do not wish me out of this or in any way seek to get me out, for I will not be got out while this trial is on. These are my people, God has given them to me, and I will live or die for Him and His glory.   – GLADYS AYLWARD

Today, my response to listening to God is:

SIMPLICITY: SEEK FIRST HIS KINGDOM
BY MARY WALLACE | SOMALIA, DJIBOUTI & ETHIOPIA

Simplicity is making the journey of life with just baggage enough.

CHARLES DUDLEY WARNER

When my husband and I left for Africa, we each carried with us two large suitcases of stuff. It seemed like few enough possessions since we had only recently owned two cars, a two-bedroom house, and a business, plus all the other trappings of American life. Those four suitcases, however, were surprisingly burdensome. Four suitcases were more than we could carry for any distance. They took up a lot of space in our lodgings. And they were filled with things we had anticipated we might need in Africa but were, instead, inappropriate. And when confronted with the poverty of most Africans, we were embarrassed by our largesse. We moved a lot during our first years on the mission field, frequently flying on airlines where the luggage allowance was one large suitcase per passenger. So we gave away some of our belongings and stashed other stuff in an attic in Nairobi, where it was chewed on by rats. We reduced our baggage to half of what we had brought from America, but it was still heavy.

In our travels we met an African evangelist in Uganda. He set for us the standard for the simple life. He carried a briefcase. Inside there was a Bible and a clean shirt; they were baggage enough for him. We were inspired, but being fond of clean underwear, socks, pajamas, pencils, books, cameras, sports shoes, flip-flops, and toiletries, we could never ever hope to duplicate his lifestyle. What did he do when his pants got dirty?

In Matthew 6:25-33, Jesus describes for us a right relationship with the material world: "Seek first his kingdom and his righteousness" and he'll take care of the rest. In his book *Celebration of Discipline,* addressing the discipline of simplicity, Richard J. Foster writes: "Everything hinges upon maintaining the 'first' thing as first. Nothing must come before the kingdom of God, including the desire for a simple lifestyle. Simplicity becomes idolatry when it takes precedence over seeking the kingdom."

Concerning the Scripture "Seek ye first God's kingdom and his righteousness," Søren Kierkegaard wrote in *Christian Discourses:* "What does this mean, what have I to do, or what sort of effort is it that can be said to seek or pursue the kingdom of God? Shall I try to get a job suitable to my talents and powers in order thereby to exert an influence? No, thou shalt *first* seek God's kingdom. Shall I then give all my fortune to the poor? No, thou shalt *first* seek God's kingdom. Shall I then go out to proclaim this teaching to the world? No, thou shalt *first* seek God's kingdom. But then in a certain sense it is nothing I shall do. Yes, certainly, in a certain sense it is nothing, become nothing before God, learn to keep silent; in this silence is the beginning, which is *first* to seek God's kingdom."

As modern Christians we live as if a tightrope were strung between "the land flowing with milk and honey" and "sell everything you have and give to the poor." We are greedy for more but need to assuage our guilt over what we have. We try to maintain a balance and call it simplicity. We risk falling into the net of idolatry either by embracing materialism and serving possessions, or by renouncing possessions and embracing legalism and asceticism. But true simplicity emanates from meditating on the words of Jesus and then following His commandments and His example. Jesus says, "Fall into freedom; trust me, and stop worrying about what you have or don't have!"

LIVE DEAD CHALLENGE

Read Matthew 6:25-33 and let it sink in. Meditate on it. Bathe in it. Shower with it. Roll in it. Spend time with it. Seek the kingdom of God and His righteousness until you find that profound silence that Kierkegaard wrote about. After the silence, ask yourself what it is God is saying to you. What does it mean to the plans you have made? What effect will you let it have on what you do and how you live this day?

SUDANESE ARAB

Sudanese Arabs number more than 22 million and are the dominant ethnic collection in Sudan. They dominate politics, economics, education, the military, and the religious aspects of the country. Arab hegemony is the biggest internal problem in Sudan as the non-Arab tribes are marginalized, excluded from real power, natural resources, and legitimate input. Sudanese Arabs are also 99 percent Muslim. There are very few believers and almost no churches—public or house-based—among them.

Every time you see Arabic script or hear something on the news about Arabs, would you loose a quick arrow prayer to God. Ask the Lord of the Harvest for a church-planting movement among the Sudanese Arabs.

Today, my response to being silent is:

SACRIFICE: CLIMB ONTO THE ALTAR
BY CHARLES PORTER | TANZANIA

Abraham answered, "God himself will provide the lamb for the burnt offering, my son." And the two of them went on together. When they reached the place God had told him about, Abraham built an altar there and arranged the wood on it. He bound his son Isaac and laid him on the altar, on top of the wood.

GENESIS 22:8-9

In 2001, six weeks after September 11, my young wife and I boarded a plane to our first assignment: the Sudan. The Sudan wasn't a stretch for me. Sure, it was scary going there, but it wasn't sacrifice. Some people, and I guess I am one of them, are naturally geared toward a more adventurous lifestyle. Wearing a white robe and a turban was like putting on a well-oiled baseball glove for me. It wasn't hard. I love learning languages; I have studied and speak some variation of five of them. As a missionary kid, I wasn't tied to American culture and I didn't have a lot of close family connections to leave behind. To be quite honest, living as an "undercover missionary" put me in an exclusive club of newly minted missions superstars. Supporters gladly engaged; money was easy to raise. People really prayed for us, believing that our lives were in imminent danger.

Sacrifice began for me when our family health challenges forced us to leave the Sudan, "my" ministry, the respect, the growing influence. Sacrifice for me meant leaving my dream of reaching the unreached, preaching as Paul to the untouched. Sacrifice for me meant living according to the principles of Scripture, to put my family above my ministry and myself. Sacrifice meant accepting that I do not save, Jesus does; that it's not my kingdom, it's His; that I am a servant, on assignment, willing to go anywhere, anytime, for His good pleasure. Sacrifice for me meant gladly and lovingly keeping my wedding vows.

Today, I'm still not done. My adopted son, Joshua, the son God promised my wife and me, was recently diagnosed with Duchenne muscular dystrophy, a terminal genetic condition with a life expectancy of 21 to 25 years of age. In a few short years, he will no longer be able to walk, barring a miracle. And once that happens, I'll again give up the exciting ministry of church planting in urban Africa to return to the United States and be a father and a husband. My sacrifice will be to return to a culture I don't know and to a place where I don't command respect because of the color of my skin; 130-degree Saharan heat does not compare.

Isaac was at least 17 as he climbed the mountain with his 117-year-old father. He knew the drill. He knew child sacrifice, especially of the eldest son, was a common local practice, yet he willingly placed himself on the altar, allowing himself to be bound by someone weaker than he. All for the love of the old man. Often, we think sacrifice is Abraham, willing to give up his only son. That is love. But I've found that I relate more to Isaac. Isaac had to willingly lie on the altar and trust his father. Isaac was the sacrifice. As am I.

LIVE DEAD CHALLENGE

How have you defined sacrifice? Is it always suffering physical death or cultural distance from your family? Where are you getting your love, your respect, your acceptance? Are you willing to give those things to the Master? What is easy for you may be sacrifice for another. Are you measuring your sacrifice by what is hard for someone else? Are you willing to be the sacrifice (as opposed to making it)?

AFAR

Northern Djibouti is home to the Afar. The Afar—an unreached Muslim people group—number about 1.5 million: 250,000 in Eritrea, 250,000 in Djibouti, and the rest in Ethiopia.

The Afar have a most unusual way of dealing with recalcitrant members of their tribe. If an Afar person does not conform to the norms of society, he is taken by boat into the Gulf of Tadjoura. A large rock is tied to him, and he is thrown into the deep to drown. After he swallows enough water to lose consciousness, he is hauled out by rope and revived. Upon recovering his life, he is asked if he will now conform to what Afar society demands. If he refuses, he is again thrown into the water, again revived, and again questioned. A second denial leads to a third dunking. If the man or woman survives being "drowned" for a third time, he or she is then considered an outcast and forever shunned by the rest of his Afar tribe. This has happened to at least one Afar believer.

Every time you see a swimming pool, a pond, a lake, a river, or a body of water, would you pray for the Muslim Afar. They are very near to the Father's heart. Pray that God would raise up a church-planting team to work among the Afar. Pray about joining that team.

Today, my response to sacrificing is:

If every Christian is already considered a missionary, then all can stay put where they are, and nobody needs to get up and go anywhere to preach the gospel...

But if our only concern is to witness where we are, how will people in unevangelized areas ever hear the gospel? The present uneven distribution of Christians and opportunities to hear the gospel of Christ will continue on unchanged.

– C. GORDON OLSON

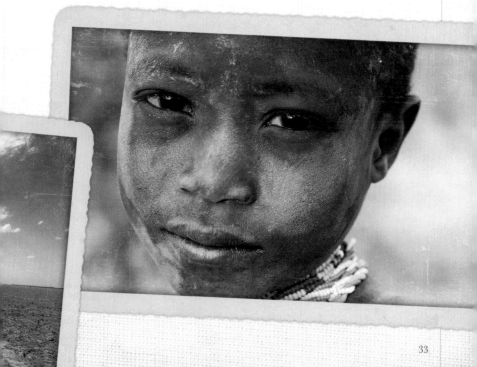

SPIRITUAL WARFARE: BATTLE IN THE UNSEEN REALM
BY GREG BEGGS | TANZANIA & KENYA

Beneath the quiet drowsiness of the little coastal Tanzanian town, something sinister stirred. Just outside my consciousness, it nagged and tugged with a relentless harassment. It put me into foul moods with an angry disposition. I lashed out at my wonderful wife for no justifiable reason. Arguments with Tanzanians, formerly not a regular occurrence, became a normal part of beleaguered days. Targeted and stalked by an invisible force that hounded our lives, we lived mostly unaware under demonic assault. Why? We were telling African Muslims about the love of Jesus.

Out of tormented sleep we would awaken to dogs howling and the syncopated rhythm of beating drums. All night the shaman would sway and mumble Swahili or Arabic mantras. Just before dawn, when all was ready, like an early morning mist, an eerie silence would settle into the darkness. As payment for services rendered, a few scrawny chickens would appear, and maybe a goat or two, depending on the severity of the need. Edicts and declarations would be made; pieces of bone, powders, or rolled-up Koranic verse would be attached to the bodies of the desperate people who had come for relief.

After the ritual, the weary and needy trudged back to humble homes to wait for the light of day and the hope that comes with the sun. Across the yard and over the hibiscus hedge, just a few hundred feet from where the shaman sat in a demonic daze, we tried to start our day with prayer.

Someone was knocking on the door. It was 6 a.m. I had not slept well. *Now what?* My attitude was a bit too surly as I welcomed my pastor friend, Ng'unda, into our home. "God woke me in the night and told me to help you," he said.

"Help me?" I replied.

"Yes," he said. "You are under a demonic attack and do not realize it or know how to fight."

I was saved and prayed every day and knew there was a devil. But that morning Pastor Ng'unda taught me new lessons about spiritual warfare, and how to pray against demonic forces of darkness. He explained to me the curse my neighbor had put on my home. And he told me why. It became clear to me that day that a world not generally recognized by natural senses really does exist. There is an unseen spiritual realm whose activity influences everyday life.

It is an extreme to have a shaman, who puts curses on you, as a neighbor. But good Christians, unaware and unequipped, face a real spirit world every day. Demonic-induced stress, temptation, relational difficulty, and other dilemmas pester believers who simply think they are having a bad day.

The Apostle Paul, in Ephesians 6:10-18, explained this to some Christians who were being attacked by the devil: "Finally, be strong in the Lord and in his mighty power. Put on the full armor of God, so that you can take your stand against the devil's schemes. For our struggle is not against flesh and blood, but against the rulers, against the authorities, against the powers of this dark world and against the spiritual forces of evil in the heavenly realms. Therefore put on the full armor of God, so that when the day of evil comes, you may be able to stand your ground, and after you have done everything, to stand. Stand firm then, with the belt of truth buckled around your waist, with the breastplate of righteousness in place, and with your feet fitted with the readiness that comes from the gospel of peace. In addition to all this, take up the shield of faith, with which you can extinguish all the flaming arrows of the evil one. Take the helmet of salvation and the sword of the Spirit, which is the word of God. And pray in the Spirit on all occasions with all kinds of prayers and requests. With this in mind, be alert and always keep on praying for all the Lord's people."

Not every problem you have is a demonic assault. We have to be balanced in our Christian walk. But how do you know? It is a good idea to pray every day for discernment and a sensitive spirit. Pray in the Spirit all the time. As you are led, pray for the Lord to bind demonic forces that hinder and harass. The more you talk to Jesus about this, the more discerning your spirit will be. And always remember, the devil and all his demons are created beings; they are not all-powerful. God is.

Living dead will require us to put aside our "tried and true" understanding of why and how things happen in life. Deny yourself a Western scientific answer for cause and effect. Humble yourself and realize that there is another world that does exist. And ask the Holy Spirit for balanced discernment so as not to get weird, seeing and blaming all problems on the demonic.

LIVE DEAD CHALLENGE

- Pray in the Spirit today as much as you can.
- Mentally put on the "whole armor of God" and apply it to your day.
- As the Holy Spirit leads you, engage in spiritual warfare by praying against the forces of evil that hold people captive and cause untold heartache in your city.

ZAGHAWA

The Zaghawa are a proud African people found in Sudan, Chad, and Libya. They number up to 350,000 and are essentially completely Muslim. In medieval times they ruled most of what is now Chad and western Sudan, and even today the president of Chad is a Zaghawa. In Sudan, the Zaghawa are known to be fierce fighters, pious about their Islamic faith, and unafraid to stand up against corruption. Their language is also called Zaghawa, and there is a breed of sheep called Zaghawa.

Every time you see a sheep, eat mutton, or drive by a farm, would you remember the Zaghawa people in prayer and ask that these lost sheep would be found by their loving and living Shepherd.

Today, my response to spiritual warfare is:

EXPECTATIONS: WHAT HAVE I SIGNED UP FOR?
BY JENNIFER BROGDEN | SUDAN

"Suppose one of you had a servant plowing or looking after the sheep. Would he say to the servant when he comes in from the field, 'Come along now and sit down to eat'? Would he not rather say, 'Prepare my supper, get yourself ready and wait on me while I eat and drink; after that you may eat and drink'? Would he thank the servant because he did what he was told to do? So you also, when you have done everything you were told to do, should say, 'We are unworthy servants; we have only done our duty.' "

LUKE 17:7-10

A wise pastor reminded us of this passage as we were first preparing to leave for Sudan. It was a timely word that I've never forgotten. Going into Sudan as Christ's servants, what did I expect of our labor there?

Looking back, I had a handful of expectations that I thought were pretty realistic: I expected it to be hot, hard, dusty and dry, resistant; I expected God to be faithful to His Word. Most of my expectations were met without delay. Daily temperatures over 105 degrees Fahrenheit for months on end, tears in my first Arabic lesson, huge walls of dust ushering in mere minutes of rainfall … and God was faithful to His Word.

He just wasn't faithful in the way I expected Him to be.

I found it discouraging that language teachers weren't interested in saying the sinner's prayer after two years of life on life with them. Neighbors were kind and hospitable but not ready for a Bible study. Thoughts of *Why am I here?* and *This isn't what I signed up for* started rapping in my brain.

Then came "What Did You Expect?"—the sermon title of a guest speaker at our field meeting. These words stuck with me the same way Luke 17 has. God had been so faithful over the years. Faithful to protect us, heal us, restore us, refresh us, get us visas. … So, what was my problem? Everything in Sudan was exactly as I had originally expected it to be. Hot, slow, difficult, daily battles in the spirit realm, conflicts within and without. Why was life such a struggle? Why couldn't I be content and satisfied?

Because I'd forgotten that it was my part just to obey, that Jesus is my just reward—that He can do as He sees fit with me, my family, and the work in Sudan. Jesus makes every night without power and every delay over visas and permits worth it. And *only* Jesus makes it worth it.

I didn't expect God to bring me all this way to change what He saw in me. But He has. I needed Sudan more than Sudan needed me, and I didn't expect that. I thought God was bringing me to Sudan to change Sudan. I did not realize that His primary purpose was to expose all the junk in my heart and change me! I'm so grateful that in the "less" of ministry, as I thought it should be, I got more than I expected.

What do you expect dying to self will feel like? Do you think it will be pleasant? Painless? Problem free? What do you expect it to feel like when you live dead? Do you expect people to understand, support you, praise you, clap for you? Do you expect the devil to cheer and every demon in hell to yield to your noble aspirations? Do you expect to be welcomed or affirmed by your peers and understood by your parents? Do you expect people to get in line to support you financially? Do you expect that your plans will be changed, your timing delayed, and your will continually crossed? Do you expect to surrender once in an air-conditioned church, kneeling on a carpeted altar with a handy box of Kleenex perkily waiting to be plucked … and then from that point on to sail without contrary winds into God's sheltered will? Or do you expect God to wring the self out of you in a painful and lengthy process using circumstance and shattered expectations—and then surprise you with how good it feels to have His image stamped deeply onto yours.

LIVE DEAD CHALLENGE

Write in your journal what you expect it means to live dead. Be as objective as you can. List your expectations. "I expect living dead to hurt." "I expect living dead to be humbling." "I expect to be underappreciated and overlooked." They don't all have to be sober. Include some expectations of faith such as, "I expect God to be faithful to His promises." "I expect Jesus to conform me into His image." Transfer this list of realistic expectations into your Bible under the heading "What did you expect?" and refer to it whenever your unmet (and unbiblical) expectations disappoint you.

Go out into this day expecting to live dead, embracing the momentary pain for the long-term joy.

SOMALI (SOMALILAND)

Many Somalis, especially the women, are oppressed or even possessed by evil spirits. One woman was struck dumb for three weeks by a spirit that troubled her. Jesus is able to cast out these evil spirits, but the Somalis have not welcomed Him to come into their lives to do so. In the absence of a true and permanent remedy, they seek to appease these spirits through various ceremonies. One woman was counseled to pop popcorn and throw some of it into each corner of her living room. Another woman was advised to drink strong black coffee every Tuesday morning. Another common remedy is to write a verse from the Koran on a piece of paper. Then the ink is washed off into a vessel and the water is drunk as medicine.

For more serious cases, a saar is performed. This ceremony is often attended by a large group of women. An animal sacrifice is made, special drummers are hired, and the afflicted women dance to the hypnotic drumbeats until they go into a trance. A spirit possesses them at this time and is supposed to help them with their original problem.

Whenever you hear a drumbeat, remember the demon-possessed women of Somalia and pray that the Lord would deliver them.

Today, my response to expectations is:

INTEGRITY IN SPEECH: BIBLICAL GUIDELINES FOR CONVERSATION
BY SCOTT HANSON | TANZANIA

In one of my favorite comic strips, "Calvin & Hobbes," Calvin is frustrated with life at home. His remedy is to secede from his family. After leaving the house, Calvin discovers that he made a poor choice and decides to return home. Hobbes reminds him that he can't go home; he has seceded. Calvin sheepishly replies, "My life needs a rewind and erase button."

Many times in life I wish I could rewind and erase an event or conversation. More often than not, the offending event has to do with talking when I should have been quiet. When I was a young missionary, a buddy of mine was talking to me about some things he had been told by a missionary colleague. I was somewhat offended by the information being discussed and chimed in that he should take what my colleague said with a grain of salt. Little did I realize the series of events that my little comment would cause. My buddy went back to the missionary and told him I had said he couldn't be trusted. My missionary colleague was upset I had bad-mouthed him, so he talked to my country coordinator. It was quite a mess. Oh, for that rewind and erase button. If I had it to do over again, I would not have given in to the temptation to talk about one of my team members. My indiscretion, although not malicious by intent and not seemingly potent in content, caused a lot of unnecessary pain.

Of course we wouldn't need the rewind-erase button if we would monitor our conversations before speaking. Ephesians 4:29 gives guidelines for appropriate conversation: "Do not let any unwholesome talk come out of your mouths, but only what is helpful for building others up according to their needs so that it might benefit those who listen."

Initially Paul addresses motivation. Why are you talking about someone else? Appropriate conversation is geared toward building others up. Before you speak, evaluate your motives and the potential outcome. Will the conversation build the person up in the hearts of those who are listening? If the person we are talking about were to walk into the conversation, would he or she feel edified? If not, then it is unwholesome talk.

Second, Paul shares that the conversation should be "according to their needs." If we are going to discuss other people, then we need to put it in the perspective of what is best for them. Is what I am saying about others benefitting them somehow? Am I concerned for someone's well being, or could even an innocent conversation put this person in a negative light?

Finally we need to be concerned about our conversation's effect on the listener. Is the conversation beneficial? Will it be edifying to them? Will it make them respect or care for our subject in a greater way, or is it subtly degrading?

When you begin to apply Paul's filters, you will find that you have far fewer rewind-erase moments. Your conversations will be both edifying to God and to your fellow human beings.

LIVE DEAD CHALLENGE

Make a vow of silence today, speaking only when absolutely necessary. Monitor the conversations around you and take note of how many of them follow the biblical pattern. Pray that God will help you to speak in a way that brings glory to Him.

For the rest of the week, before every conversation, take a moment to run through a quick checklist: Is it beneficial? Is it focused on the needs of others? Is it edifying to the listener? If you have any reservations, choose not to speak.

SHAGIYYA

The Shagiyya Arabs are known to be the most cunning. Their neighboring tribes have a proverb: "Lau talga shagi wa dabi fii tarriq, uktul ash-shagi wa khali ad-dabi." Translated, it means, "If you find a snake and a Shagiyya in the road, kill the Shagiyya and leave the snake." One of the largest subsets of the Northern Sudanese Arabs, the Shagiyya excel at business and in the military. Their heartland is in northern Sudan along the Nile, both north and south of the Town of Atbarra. The Shagiyya are Muslims, and there are very few believers among them.

Pray for the Shagiyya people. Pray for the team forming to reach them. Pray about joining the team. Every time you see a snake—live, in a book or magazine, or on television—pray for the Shagiyya people.

Today, my response to biblical conversation is:

PASSION: LIVE THE WAY JESUS INTENDED
BY ANGUS BLACK | SOUTH AFRICA, BURUNDI, DJIBOUTI & MADAGASCAR

I remember taking a morning walk with my wife, Joan, down the dusty streets of Bujumbura, Burundi. We listened to the machine-gun fire between the rebel forces and government troops only a few kilometers away in Buterere. Usually the fighting took place at night, maybe around 9 p.m., when the rebel forces would attack the city. Fighting in broad daylight, especially this close to the capital, was not normal. But then again, nothing about living in Burundi was normal for me.

Some missionaries thrive on great tales of adventure: Rebel forces! AK-47s! Grenade blasts! The stuff of powerful, tear-jerking newsletters. But not me. You see, I'm a farm kid, not a Navy SEAL or a Special Forces tough guy. I relish peace and quiet. Thus, I found myself devoid of life, without passion, as the realities of living in this war-torn country overwhelmed me and threatened to completely gut me emotionally and spiritually. The constant police checks with demands for bribes, the never-ending remnants of civil war, even the corruption at the post office—it all drained me beyond words. And what about my wife and four young children? How could I protect them in such an environment? I couldn't. There was no way. Did I make a mistake by bringing them into this violent country?

I had one of two choices to make: quit or find a way to cope. Yeah, I know, neither option sounds very spiritual, but if I couldn't recapture some passion again, I was finished.

I sought God daily in Bible reading and intense prayer, well-known "spiritual" activities. Yet, I still felt completely drained. So I began, as a matter of strict discipline, working out with Joan. It wasn't about getting a six-pack; rather, it was all about restoring passion. And, although we typically love dramatic films, we only watched clean, silly comedies. We laughed so hard. Serious films were not allowed. Every day we got outside of our razor-wired walls to literally soak in the sunshine. We dusted off our favorite hobbies, spent more time playing games as a family, and found ways to laugh and enjoy life. I also avoided, within reason, some life-draining activities. This change of lifestyle proved amazingly refreshing, almost miraculous. My challenges didn't go away, but my passion for life and ministry slowly began to return. We serve God best as passion-filled people. And we die best when our lives overflow with passion. *We die well only as we learn to live well.* The better we live—exuberantly, joyfully, passionately—the more we can truly *live dead.*

Jesus Christ, the ultimate Life Giver and our source of passion, talks about life: "The thief's purpose is to steal and kill and destroy. My purpose is to give life in all its fullness" (John 10:10, NLT). Satan renders us ineffective in our service to the Life Giver when he finds a way to drain the passion from our lives. And not just "spiritual" passion, but the "mundane" zest we so desperately need in our daily activities. Jesus, however, gives us life "in all its fullness." Pause and think about the phrase in all its fullness. We often compartmentalize our lives into "spiritual" and "nonspiritual" activities, even if we do it subtly and subconsciously, but Jesus never asks or expects us to do that. He breathes life into us in all its fullness, comprehensively and completely! If we play sports, we should play hard. If we're musicians, we should create heavenly music. If we love photography, we should search for the perfect moment with perfect lighting. If we're coffee lovers, we should drink good coffee with gusto. Only a passion-filled person can live dead; a passionless person cannot.

Lord, help me to live each day with passion, for in living well, I am humbly opening myself to the challenge to live dead.

LIVE DEAD CHALLENGE

We all have some life-draining people or activities in our lives. Some cannot be avoided, but others, quite honestly, can. Take a few moments asking God to show you areas that unnecessarily drain life from you. Now, muster the courage to cut out one life-draining issue in your life this week. To live dead does not mean to live in misery. Even in the midst of great challenges, we can live with passion—not in a phony, superficial way, but with a quiet and profound trust in the Life Giver.

Now list three life-giving activities, things that truly refresh you, regardless of how mundane each may be. Then write out an action plan to incorporate at least one of the activities into your weekly schedule for the next month. Resist the temptation to feel guilty about doing "nonspiritual" activities. Rather, get out of bed each morning and live each day to the fullest, the way Jesus intended.

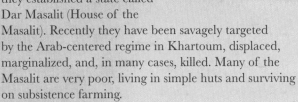

MASALIT

The Masalit are a Muslim people of Darfur in western Sudan (170,000) and Wadai in eastern Chad (67,000). They speak Masalit, a Nilo-Saharan language of the Maba group. Between 1884 and 1921, they established a state called Dar Masalit (House of the Masalit). Recently they have been savagely targeted by the Arab-centered regime in Khartoum, displaced, marginalized, and, in many cases, killed. Many of the Masalit are very poor, living in simple huts and surviving on subsistence farming.

Every time you are treated unfairly, every time you hear about a bully, every time you read about some injustice at home or around the world, would you remember the long-suffering Masalit people of Darfur, Sudan, and ask the God of Justice to justify many of the Masalit before God.

Today, my response to living with passion is:

I had utterly abandoned myself to Him. Could any choice be as wonderful as His will?

Could any place be safer than the center of His will? Did not he assure me by His very presence that His thoughts toward us are good, and not evil? Death to my own plans and desires was almost deliriously delightful. Everything was laid at His nail-scarred feet, life or death, health or illness, appreciation by others or misunderstanding, success or failure as measured by human standards. Only He himself mattered. – V. RAYMOND EDMAN

PERSECUTION: 'I AM WITH YOU ALWAYS'
BY KEVIN SMITH | SOMALIA, ERITREA, DJIBOUTI & KENYA

Consider it pure joy, my brothers, whenever you face trials of many kinds.

JAMES 1:2

Thomas* was one of the Bible-school students we taught in Eritrea. He was an amazing evangelist. Everywhere he went, people came to Jesus. One day he was forcefully drafted into the military. Security officials took him to a training camp, took away his Bible, forced him to stop praying with others, and told him to stop witnessing. Thomas wouldn't stop witnessing, even after being threatened by his commanders. He dared to tell them what Jesus could do for them! Finally they imprisoned him and tortured him, hoping to shut him up. They pushed him face down in the dirt, took a wire cord, tied his arms to his legs behind his back in a figure eight, and wrenched him into agonizing pain. They left him like that in the blazing sun for hours. The cord cut off his blood circulation, and in three hours his lower arm swelled to four times its normal size. Days later, gangrene set in, and the doctors decided they had to amputate to save his life. Just before the operation, the infection burst through his skin, rendering his fingers permanently immobile and leaving a huge scar on his forearm.

Many others like Thomas are tortured to force their denial of Jesus. They have refused, stating: "No, I will not give Him up. Jesus died for me; now I will die for him!" These men and women are powerful. Why? We believe it is because of the words of Jesus in Matthew 28:20: "I am with you always, even to the end of the age." Power in persecution comes from intimacy with Jesus, a sense of nearness that is felt most keenly in the hour of persecution.

Another brother, Matthew, described to me the horrors of being imprisoned for more than two years in a metal shipping container in Assab, a port town on the Red Sea. Heat indexes reached 140 degrees Fahrenheit, and he would bake inside that container. He was thrown a dry piece of bread and granted only a tiny cup of water each day. Once a day he was let out to relieve himself on the sparse, desert ground, suffering humiliation while his torturers looked on, mocking and jeering, asking him where his Jesus was now. With tears in my eyes, I wondered out loud how he could have borne such persecution.

Matthew leaned across the table, half-standing with his face close to mine, and said, "Kevin, never have I felt so close to Jesus as when he was with me in that prison!"

The power in persecution is the presence of Jesus Christ Himself!

Harun, the leader of the national church, knew his days of freedom were numbered, so he began to teach his children what it means to be persecuted and how Christians are to respond. His kids were the same age as my own: 8, 5, and 2 years. Early one morning before the sun rose, soldiers came to his house and took him away. John, his 5-year-old son, was the first to wake up. When he realized Daddy was gone, he cried and wailed so loudly that his 8-year-old sister, Salome, was awakened. Putting her arms around her younger brother, she comforted him, saying, "No, John, no! Father taught us to count it all *joy* to suffer for Jesus. We must not cry; we must shout for joy!" Salome let out a yell that morning that could not and will not be overcome by any demonic power. We have much to learn from 8-year-old Salome's faith in an ever-present Jesus. "I am with you always!"

Harun has been imprisoned since 2004 and has not been home to see his children grow. His last words to me were, "Kevin, ask our brothers and sisters to pray for us; not that we should be free from this persecution, but that we will stand up boldly under it and proclaim Christ as we should."

LIVE DEAD CHALLENGE

It is humbling to personally know believers who have been and are continually tortured, persecuted, and imprisoned for loving Jesus and refusing to stop living out their love for Him. Today, Marxist Eritrea is one of the most difficult countries to access with the gospel. Would you spend time today praying for Eritrea?

Pray for the persecuted believers there who continue to bravely suffer for Jesus. Pray that God would send missionaries to the unreached peoples of Eritrea. In what ways are you embarrassed of Christ? Look today for some way you can stand up for Him. Ask Jesus if He would grace you with the opportunity to suffer for His name today.

Editor's note: Names of Eritrean believers have been changed for the protection of their families.

NUBIANS

The Nubians of northern Sudan and southern Egypt are the descendants of the great kingdom of Kush. Kush was a powerful kingdom in Old Testament times, ruling Egypt (the Black Pharaohs of the 25th dynasty). And under Taharqa, they even pushed up into Israel to confront the Assyrians. Moses' second wife, the man who rescued Jeremiah from the miry clay, the runner (poor man) who got outrun to take David news, and, of course, the eunuch of Acts 8 fame—all were Nubians. African Christianity, in fact, was Nubian-born.

By the 15th century Islam had overrun the Christian kingdoms of Nubia, and by the 20th century almost all traces of Christianity were covered by sand. But not all. Nubians still take their newborns to the river and make the sign of the cross in water on their foreheads. When asked why, they shrug and say, "We don't know. That is what our ancestors did."

Nubians are proud of their heritage, and the Nubian gate is distinct and ornate. **Every time you knock on a door, would you pray that the door of Nubian hearts would be opened again to the Savior they have neglected and forgotten.**

Today, my response to persecution is:

ABANDON: ONE LIFE TO GIVE
BY AMY CLEVELAND | SOMALIA

Editor's note: The chapters for Days 10 and 11 are written by a couple who has worked among Somalis in the United States for 15 years. They now are assigned to Somalia. I asked the wife if she really understood the cost and implications of living in Somalia. Was she really ready to die? Was she ready to live the rest of her life a widow? Was she ready to leave her three children as orphans? What follows are some excerpts from her response.

"For whoever desires to save his life will lose it, but whoever loses his life for my sake will find it."

MATTHEW 16:25

You asked how I feel about the dangers—the possibilities of harm and death—that could be involved in following through on this calling.

In prayer I cry with Jesus over these matters, over the ramifications on our children, on my husband, on me, on our marriage, on the work. We cry together. Jesus speaks to me comfortingly, "All die." I know that these words may not comfort all, but they comfort me. They mean so much to me, these two words. They give me such peace. They humble me. They bring me clarity. They ground me with perspective for living well.

We do not live free from pressure. We feel "watched." I am not always sure whom to trust in the community. I have had nightmares here of what could happen. I have picked up the phone and heard shouting in Somali. I have been chased down the street by a Somali man clearly asking from me what he never should have asked. I have friends who have been harassed by Somalis. We have American friends who constantly misunderstand us and wish we'd forget about these Somalis. It affects the clothes I wear and what my young daughters wear. These are only some examples.

I don't think we pay too high a price.

I feel what I can do is obey. I feel what I can do is trust God. I feel what I can do is walk with the Lord. We do all die. We have one life then to live, to give. One life. How could I do anything but that to which I am called?

I am the bride of Christ! What joyful life do I have if not to take my children where my Lord brings me? For me there is no choice or thought of choice. I am His.

There is much to fear. Things I can think of cause me to tremble, and things I know I cannot think of bring me much trembling. I know there are costs. Some costs I can see and some I know I don't see yet or never will. As I take my mind to Jesus, I lose the fears. I find peace that doesn't originate with me and goes deep enough for me to stand in. I find joy in His leading and in what He is leading me into. I can begin to see how my great Lord is piecing many things together and considering all our needs and desires as well.

Death is so normal. Death touches all. Death often comes unannounced. I cannot control it nor will I be ruled by some irrational fear of it. What fools who do! I most likely won't know it is coming. It could come today or tomorrow. Harm, the same.

I feel that God is doing something great in our lives. I dream to live long and peacefully and joyfully in Somalia; to lead and to establish, to rise with the empowerment of Jesus to the unbelievable tasks ahead. I intend to make a home that exalts Christ in all things. I intend to lead my children in joy. I intend to love my husband here long and well.

I do hope God isn't leading us to die in Somalia at the hands of hatred. But I will not be ruled by that possibility and I feel I would be a fool to think that my life anywhere is free from death. I hope that God's work in my heart is not a sign of what we must face. Even so, I see it as a terrible (meaning huge and strong) privilege to serve God among these lost. And I surrender with great joy to His plan, trusting however He plans to sow our lives.

LIVE DEAD CHALLENGE

Spend some time reflecting on your own physical death. Are you ready? Do you see it as an end or a beginning? Are you prepared to answer the call of Jesus to an unreached people of the world if it means you or someone in your family dies? Is Jesus worth dying for? Are you willing to die for Jesus? If Jesus called you to work among a dangerous people group like the Somalis, or the Taliban, or Hezbollah, or Hamas, would you do it? Would you take your family there? If you knew you would die this evening, how would you live today? Go out and live today in that spirit.

UNREACHED PEOPLE GROUP

DJIBOUTI SOMALI

The Somalis' favorite food is milk, any kind of milk, but especially camel milk. The camels are milked by the men, who stand on one leg and raise the other so that their thigh is horizontal to the ground. This makes a platform on which they set the finely woven basket into which they squirt the camel's milk.

The Somali word *maal* means "to milk." Adding the particle *soo* makes it reflexive—that is, *soo maal* means "milk for yourself." When the people in the bush received a guest, they would express their hospitality by telling them "soo maal," that is, feel so welcome and at home that you would milk my camel for yourself anytime you want. This traditional statement of hospitality eventually became the name for the people themselves—Somali.

Whenever you drink milk, think of Somali hospitality and say a prayer for them to welcome our Lord Jesus with this traditional warmth.

Today, my response to physical death is:

PROPHECY: SEEING AND DECLARING
BY WILL CLEVELAND | SOMALIA

"I will pour out my Spirit on all flesh; your sons and your daughters shall prophesy."

JOEL 2:28 (ESV)

Let me give you a basic definition of prophecy: seeing and declaring God's perspective.

Prophecy starts with knowing God's perspective. But God says, "My thoughts are not your thoughts neither are your ways my ways" (Isaiah 55:8, ESV), which means if you or I do see something from God's perspective it's only because He has opened our blind eyes (2 Corinthians 4:4, ESV) and given us a spirit of revelation to know Him (Ephesians 1:17, ESV). And that's designed to keep us humble; otherwise, we'd be so full of ourselves for "seeing God's perspective" that we'd scarcely have any room left for His perspective in our lives.

But prophecy is not complete without some form of declaration or proclamation of what you have seen. And often it's not popular, which makes sense since something that is popular is liked, admired, or enjoyed by humankind in general—and God's not a human.

These days, it's popular to say, "Somalia is a hopeless situation." It's less popular to say, "Even if Somalia is hopeless, we should still try to help." It's anti-popular to say, "Because God loves Somalis and Somalia, I am going there."

Things are this way because most of Somalia is controlled by competing guns. Whether wielded by government forces, Islamic militias, or neighborhood kids, the guns thunder only chaos and destruction, never the promised peace. Violence is as regular as it is unpredictable, which means the only thing you can count on is a daily game of Russian roulette with death. It's not hard to understand why people have a tendency to say, "Leave Somalia to Somalis. … We will come back maybe in 50 years when they really want to settle their problems."

But Christians cannot wait for things to get better in Somalia before we go there. If we do, we will forfeit a perfect opportunity to proclaim Christ. Think about this: God didn't wait for you to get your life together before He demonstrated His love for you. "God shows his love for us in that while we were still sinners, Christ died for us" (Romans 5:8, ESV). God's love is so amazing precisely because He loves His enemies and has proved it by Christ's living with them, serving them, and then dying at their hands.

It wasn't safe for Jesus to love you; it was deadly. And Jesus isn't bluffing when He commands Christians to "love our enemies" (Matthew 5:44, ESV). He knows exactly what He's asking of us. Where are the prophets who will stand up to the popular idea of safety and call God's people to safety in the arms of Jesus, whether in life or death? The stage is set in shattered Somalia. Somalis are watching as the curtain rises. God forbid that the Bride of Christ misses her cue.

LIVE DEAD CHALLENGE

One important way to engage in an act of prophecy is to submit to the Lord's dealings in your own life. As God shows you His perspective about something in your life, you can pray, "God, change me, and change the hearts of this unreached people in the same way you are changing me." That's a prophetic prayer.

Is this whole Live Dead challenge really difficult for you? Do you feel resistance to it in your heart? Are you scared of failing? Let me prophesy to you: "While we were still weak, at the right time Christ died for the ungodly" (Romans 5:6, ESV).

BEJA

The Beja are a Hamitic and nomadic people that roam the deserts of northeastern Sudan. They love their camels and their coffee and are known to be fierce competitors. They are in fact the only people on record who were brave enough to break the famed British military square. Their warriors dove under the bellies of the cavalry and ripped open the horses' stomachs with their short stout spears. The Beja have a dark complexion and large combed-out Afros. When Rudyard Kipling traveled through Sudan at the turn of the 20th century, he encountered the Beja and allegedly penned the children's rhyme, "Fuzzy Wuzzy was a bear, Fuzzy Wuzzy had no hair."

The Beja number more than a million persons combined in Sudan, Egypt, and Eritrea. Every time you see a teddy bear, or every time you drink a cup of coffee, would you remember to pray for the Beja. Pray that they would become fiercely loyal to the Lord of angel armies; pray that they would become brave representatives of the King.

Today, my response to prophecy is:

TRANSPARENCY: TEAR DOWN THE WALLS
BY CHRIS SHEEP | COMOROS

My family and I live and work on a small tropical island in the Indian Ocean that happens to be 99 percent Islamic. We're surrounded by people who are antagonistic to our faith, and yet most are excited about our friendship. How should we live with transparency among them? How can we best display Jesus to the community around us?

God's Word says: "You are the light of the world. A city set on a hill cannot be hidden; nor does anyone light a lamp and put it under a basket, but on a lampstand, and it gives light to all who are in the house. Let your light shine before men in such a way that they may see your good works, and glorify your Father who is in heaven" (Matthew 5:14-16).

For us, transparency means no walls, no dogs, and open doors. We want to be bright lights in this dark land, and so we've chosen to live "in community." Is it easy … comfortable … fun? No, most of the time it's not. It takes dying constantly and I'm not very good at that—but God is my strength. So all sorts of people come by to greet us, to demand cold water, to borrow hair clippers or the blender, to get a cup of sugar or some oil. Still others come when we're eating. In this culture, generosity and hospitality are prized, and sharing food is pretty much compulsory, so we invite them to our table.

Here's how it played out one night. My wife, Beka, was off teaching women's aerobics and I was home with our four young sons and a guest from overseas. Beka left us with a pot of soup to warm up, and we'd bought some bread, plenty of food for the six of us. We sat down to eat and one by one the visitors started to come. We welcomed them to sit down with us. Six became eight. Eight became ten, and still the visitors came. We found more chairs, brought out more plates and cups and spoons and dished out what we had (and God seemed to miraculously multiply it). By the time my sweaty, tired, and hungry wife got home from aerobics, there were 13 of us guys crowded around the table. The soup and bread were gone (and I'm guessing all the cold water was too). My wonderful wife rolled with it, found something else to eat, and joined us as we all bonded around the table in a hot dining room.

So what happens in a situation like that?

- Our islander friends see us pray and thank God for the meal.
- The boys and I get to serve … hopefully, "service with a smile."
- Friendships develop and grow around the table.
- Some of our guests stay on and observe family devotions after the meal.
- We get to shine our lights and die to ourselves.

Paul said he had such an affection for the Thessalonians that he was well-pleased to impart to them not only the gospel of God, but *also his own life* because they were so dear to him (1 Thessalonians 2:8). That's the way I want to be: joyfully serving out of love, and not just serving out of duty. I miss that mark quite often. I'm decently good at forcing myself to do "the right thing," but cheerful giving is more elusive. The good news is that God is slowly changing my heart, and there are times when my giving is cheerful and my service is from a heart of love. He is changing me to be more godly… more like Him.

Relational transparency with the community around us—that's important, but let's go to a deeper level. How about personal heart transparency and vulnerability? How many of us are living with walls around our hearts, sins concealed, and façades erected? James tells us to "confess our sins to one another and pray for one another, so that you may be healed" (5:16). David says that when he kept silent about his sin, his body wasted away (Psalm 32:3). It's so totally freeing to open up and become transparent. All of us are sinners. Why do we often try to pretend we're not? And unconfessed sin blocks our prayers. Isaiah says, "But your iniquities have made a separation between you and your God, and your sins have hidden His face from you *so that He does not hear*" (59:2).

Two of my colleagues and I teach English in the local prison every Wednesday morning. People are literally walled in, separated from community, and living in shame. Some of us may not be in a real concrete prison, but sin and hiding have put us in bondage in our hearts. Open up! Admit where you've been wrong. Tell others where they're right. Say you're sorry. And be free! For me, that means apologizing when I've been too overbearing with the kids. Or admitting that my attitude stinks in a particular area. Or calling someone and asking forgiveness for saying too much to others about his or her personal issue. Read Psalm 51, David's confession of sin and his desire to return to the joy of his salvation (verse 12).

LIVE DEAD CHALLENGE

Transparency and openness go completely against so much that is naturally fallen within us. Our carnal selves want to be guarded and hide our faults and feign that all is well. Here's the challenge: Pray and ask God to show you *anything* in your life that needs to be confessed. Determine who you will confess it to and when. Put the plan in writing in your calendar or in your journal. When you do confess, be sure to take time to pray together, and *be healed* (James 5:16).

Now for the second challenge. Are you living "in community"? Are you sharing your life and possessions with others? Can people borrow your car? Or your computer? As I like to ask my 5-year-old son when he comes home from kindergarten, "Do you share your snack?" Think of something in your life that you hold too tightly and tear down the wall.

Here I am,
send me.

—ISAIAH

FUR

The Fur people are the largest ethnic group in the western Sudan region of Darfur. In fact, Darfur means *home of the Fur.* Traditionally they live in small villages (governed by village elders) growing grain crops, although some raise livestock. The competition for agricultural land and water rights has produced tension in the region. The war in Darfur, which began in 2003, has led to a massive diaspora of the Fur people ranging from Chad in the west to camps for internally displaced people around Khartoum in the east.

The Fur people are devout Muslims but still cling to their African heritage. They love music, dance, and storytelling, which easily shifts into dramatic reenactments.
There are nearly a million Fur people, with very few, if any, known evangelicals and less than 5 percent professing Christians (according to Joshua Project data).

Pray for the Fur people today any time you read in the newspaper about conflict or sense conflict, either internally or between people. The Fur people have been widely scattered because of the conflict in Darfur. As a result, they may have more exposure to the gospel than at any time in history. In particular, this is happening as they encounter southern Sudanese Christians in Khartoum. In classic style, the Lord is bringing about good from evil.

Today, my response to being open is:

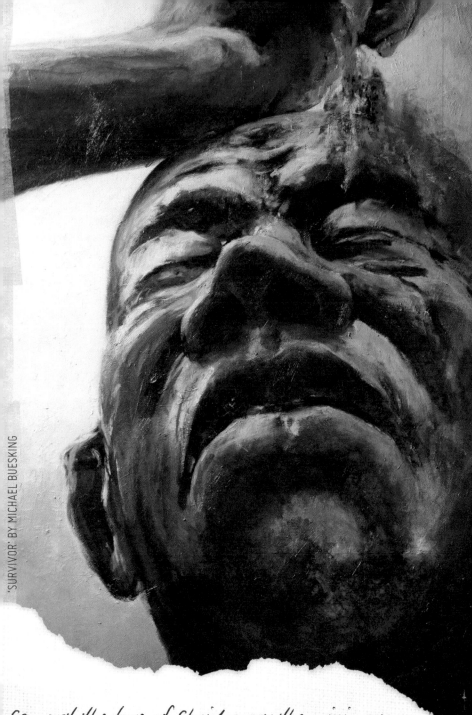

'SURVIVOR' BY MICHAEL BUESKING

Cannot the love of Christ carry the missionary where the slave-trade carries the trader?

– DAVID LIVINGSTONE

Live Dead in East Africa

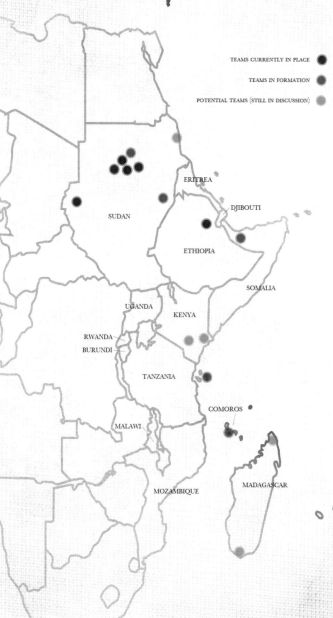

TEAMS CURRENTLY IN PLACE

TEAMS IN FORMATION

POTENTIAL TEAMS (STILL IN DISCUSSION)

ERITREA

DJIBOUTI

SUDAN

ETHIOPIA

SOMALIA

UGANDA

KENYA

RWANDA

BURUNDI

TANZANIA

COMOROS

MALAWI

MOZAMBIQUE

MADAGASCAR

AFFIRMATION: PUTTING OTHERS FIRST
BY LORETTA WIDEMAN | ETHIOPIA & KENYA

[David] said to his men, "The Lord forbid that I should do such a thing to my master, the Lord's anointed, or lift my hand against him; for he is the anointed of the Lord."

1 SAMUEL 24:6

His name is David. The guy is brilliant. When you read what he's written, you think, *Wow. I wish I had said that.* In meetings where everyone is trying to get a word in, David quietly watches, listens, and then when he speaks, it's a masterpiece, a word of wisdom.

David lives in one of those countries in East Africa where few are willing to go. The place where he lives is hot. It's dirty. In this country you can watch as a candle sadly leans over backward—or forward, depending on the way you're looking at it—as the wick makes a slow downward dive.

What's so special about David? Besides his brilliance, humility, and commitment to serve God in difficult places, he is willing to put others first, to affirm his colleagues. He prays for workers in the harvest field and then encourages them. He doesn't have to be number one. So many times we pray and pray that God would send workers to help us, and then when they come, instead of affirming and focusing on the positive, we tend to get caught up in relational issues. I listened in our committee meeting as David affirmed the leader, a man years younger than himself. Instead of jealousy or intimidation, David chose to appreciate his colleague's obvious gifts and contributions to the team.

This David reminds me of another David we read about in the Bible. David, son of Jesse, knew he was a chosen man. God had given him power and favor. But someone he had trusted was trying to kill him. As he crept up and found Saul asleep in the cave, he cut off a corner of Saul's robe. We might say, "Serves him right!" David, however, knew he had done wrong. He had lifted his hand against the Lord's anointed. How many times do we conjure up ideas of how we can get even, only to sense that nudging from the Holy Spirit that says, "Don't touch the Lord's anointed." When we are in competition with each other, we are working against ourselves. We are working against other people God has called for His purpose.

Affirming others doesn't sound like it would be that difficult to do, does it? We all have people we love and admire, and many of us don't have a problem giving out praise now and then. But what about the moments when we are betrayed by those we love—or even by someone we don't like very much. During those times, something rises within us and we put up our defenses.

I believe that one of the main reasons we fail in our endeavors to serve is because we are not living dead. We are still trying to protect ourselves. We need to prove our worth. We need to succeed. If we're full of ourselves, we're not dead. Only by emptying out our wants, our needs, and our obsessive desire to be better than others can we really start living dead. When we've got to have our way no matter the cost, we can be assured that we're very much alive in ourselves.

I know I am often tested when I tell the Lord I want His way—not mine. Usually, these challenges come through relationships. Someone else gets the glory for something I've done, or some other trivial event. If I really think that other guy is better than I am, if I genuinely consider her better than myself, well, wouldn't I want that other person to receive the glory? You can see the challenge. It must be a constant prayer—but one also has to take action in other ways. When we are genuinely affirming others by a word or by something we do, we chisel away a little of ourselves. The dying process begins. I would even go so far as to say the dying gets easier as we continue with the tool in hand.

LIVE DEAD CHALLENGE

One way to die to ourselves is to lift others up. Try it. Find three people that make you feel uncomfortable or demean you, and first of all pray about how you can sincerely affirm them. Then take a step to give them that affirmation by something you say or do.

Additionally, find one person who may be doing better than you—someone who has excelled to a point where you feel threatened or maybe even a little envious. Again, take a step to affirm that person with a sincere heart. Begin removing all competitive thinking from your language and vocabulary. I think you will find that a chiseling process will be taking place. You will begin to live dead.

YEMENI ARAB

There are about 65,000 Yemeni Arabs living in Djibouti. Many live in large houses with several generations and assorted relatives living under the same roof. The house is divided so visitors won't encounter members of the opposite sex. The rooms usually have some type of carpeting, and when entering the house, one must leave his or her shoes at the door. There is a men's salon and a women's salon where visitors are entertained. The salon walls are lined with upholstered mattresses and cushions to sit on and lean against. In the center of the room is a hookah (water pipe), with a long rubber hose that reaches around the room for communal tobacco smoking.

Every time you take off your shoes or sit on the floor, please remember the Yemeni Arabs of Djibouti. Pray that they would fall at the feet of King Jesus and accept Him as Lord and Savior. Pray about becoming part of a church-planting team to this precious people.

Today, my response to affirmation is:

A LEARNING HEART: THE CALL TO BE MORE
BY STEVE PENNINGTON | ETHIOPIA & KENYA

Do your best to present yourself to God as one approved, a workman who does not need to be ashamed and who correctly handles the word of truth.

2 TIMOTHY 2:15

We're a pretty relaxed generation. The thought of "doing our best" can mean a million different things to us—pushing fewer buttons on the remote, cramming fewer chips into our yawning faces, trying to enjoy or, minimally, to stay awake in the church service (even when it shatters the predetermined one-hour length), taking the stairs instead of the elevator. But, what did it mean to Timothy? The man who led him to Christ, nurtured him in the faith, trained him for ministry, and placed him in the pastorate in Ephesus encourages him: "Timothy, take this thing seriously. Do all you can to present yourself to God in a way that pleases Him. Work at it with all your heart and all your being." These words spank our ears with their foreign sounds. It's not that we don't have passion. It's not that we don't crave transcendence. It just seems so ... ordinary.

In a recent e-mail exchange with a close friend, I wrote, "Man, when I grow up I want to be just like you." He replied simply, "Be more." Be more? That's it! That's what Paul is telling Timothy. Be more. Laziness and lethargy are the twin, ugly stepsisters of our fallen nature. But, following Christ demands of us: "Be more!"

When we first arrived in Ethiopia, I was assigned to teach a class at the Addis Ababa Bible College. It was a moment of excitement mixed with fear. Here I stood before a crowd of 40-plus Ethiopians, most with graying temples and weathered faces. As the young American missionary I was supposed to have all the answers, at the ripe old age of 32. Oh yeah, intimidation—the other ugly stepsister; they were triplets.

I asked the class, "How many of you have been jailed for your faith?" Nearly every hand in the room went straight up. I spoke no Amharic at the time, so I thought they must have misunderstood my American English. I tried it again from a different syntactical angle. Same response. One more time.

Same response. Finally, an exasperated young man in the front row politely asked me, "Brother Steve, are you asking how many of us spent time in prison because we are believers in Jesus?" "Yes! That's it, that's what I'm asking," I joyfully retorted. He turned and spoke in what sounded like tongues for a few moments … a pause … then nearly every hand in the room went into the air. Be more.

The call to the nations demands it of us. We cannot escape the conviction that following Christ compels us to uncompromising excellence in our normal Christian lives. But, when you are called to represent the King of Heaven in the nations of the earth—be more! What does that practically mean? Are you passionate for the Word? Be more! Are you seeking His face in daily prayer and worship? Be more! Are you studying the culture of those you are called to serve? Be more! Do you struggle daily to speak the language of another just so you can tell him about Jesus? Be more! It never ends. We never eclipse the need to be more for Him. It's a lifelong endeavor, a wonderful journey that He takes with us.

LIVE DEAD CHALLENGE

I once heard Leonard Ravenhill say, "This generation needs to learn to eat less, sleep less, and pray more." Being more for Christ, learning-for-life, is an attitude. But it's an attitude that demands we actually do something in order to achieve it. I keep a running record of my New Year's resolutions. I've had one on there for a long time. "Expand your prayer time." Every year I looked at that unchecked box and whispered to myself: "This is it. This is the year I expand my prayer time." Every year I wrote it again. It's not that I wasn't praying. I was. I am. But the call demands more. About a month ago I came to a conclusion, *If you're going to do this, you need to wake up earlier.* Check! Wow, that was a no-brainer. Discipline requires action. How has Christ framed the command for you to "do your best to present yourself to God as one approved"? What do you need to do to be more?

BAGGARA

The Sudanese Baggara are the bad boys of Sudan. They made up the bulk of the Mahdi's army in the 1890s. They oversaw much of the recent slave raiding into southern Sudan, and they have been involved in some of the recent bloodshed in Darfur. Mounted on horses and sweeping in to attack and abduct, they have been the cause of great fear. They are a Muslim people group with very few believers. The Baggara in Sudan include several sub-tribes, such as the Rizeigat, Ta'isha, Beni Halba, and Habbaniya in Darfur; Messiria Zurug, Messiria Humur, Hawazma, and Awlad Himayd in Kordofan; and Beni Selam on the White Nile.

Every time you see a horse, would you remember to pray for the Baggara people of Sudan. Pray that Jesus would ride in to their hearts in glory and sweep them off their feet.

Today, my response to discipline is:

SERVANTHOOD: LEADING THROUGH HUMILITY
BY NATE LASHWAY | MADAGASCAR

"I have set you an example that you should do as I have done for you. I tell you the truth, no servant is greater than his master, nor is a messenger greater than the one who sent him."

JOHN 13:15-16 (NIV)

It is Sunday morning in Madagascar. Rija arrives early and grabs a broom. He begins to sweep around the church, preparing for a busy Sunday. Soon more than a thousand Malagasy believers will begin to fill this building to overflowing. Rija finishes sweeping the church and heads outside and begins to sweep and mop the simple drop toilets that are so common in Madagascar. The smells are horrific and the messes can be pretty bad. A church deacon approaches and asks if he can take the broom and finish the job. Rija politely refuses. "This is my job," he says. "I do not mind." Soon the toilets are clean and rinsed out and Rija can put away his broom. He washes his hands and then straightens his tie. Picking up his Bible, he makes his way to the front of the church to begin to greet the early arrivers and to collect his thoughts for the message he will soon deliver. Rija is not the custodian; he is the pastor. He is also the former general superintendent and one of the most powerful pastors in the Malagasy church.

As I had coffee with him in his home recently, I asked him why he takes it upon himself to clean the toilets each week, especially in a culture where respect and honor are so important. He quietly replied, "My brother, if Jesus as the Son of God could wash the disciples' feet, I can surely clean the toilets. Someone has to do it. Why not me? I was not always like this, but the older I get, the more I realize the need to model servanthood to others."

As I reflect on the story of Jesus washing the disciples' feet in John 13, I am always struck by verses 3 to 5: "Jesus knew that the Father had put all things under his power, and that he had come from God and was returning to God; so he got up from the meal, took off his outer clothing, and wrapped a towel around his waist. After that, he poured water into a basin and began to wash his disciples' feet." The humility of Jesus is amazing. How could He be such a servant? I think the key is found in verse 3. He could serve the disciples because He knew who He was. We find that Jesus knew where He stood with the Father. He knew very well He was the Son of God. Nothing could change that. And that knowledge allowed Him to take off the respected robes of authority as a teacher of the Scriptures and pick up the towel of a servant. That same knowledge allowed Him to walk the hill to Calvary and offer His life as a ransom for many, the ultimate act of servanthood.

PRAYER

Lord, help me to put aside my agenda for Yours. Give me Your heart for others. Help me to know who I am in You and walk daily in confidence as a child of God. Give me opportunities to serve.

LIVE DEAD CHALLENGE

The Live Dead initiative is all about dying to self. Do you know who you are in Christ? Do you realize that no one can take that away from you? Knowing that you are a son or daughter of God, are you willing to put it all down for advancing the gospel? Practice serving. Look for ways to serve with purpose. Let service become a part of your personality. Grab a broom, clean a toilet, help a stranger, lay down your priorities and seek God's. Live Dead is not about you. It's about them— the lost.

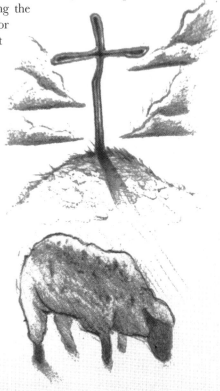

SWAHILI OF PEMBA

The island of Pemba off the coast of Tanzania is known for its exotic spices. The Pembans export cardamom, cinnamon, vanilla, cloves, and other spices. Coastal Swahili food is full of flavor. One of the island's specialties is pilau—a rice dish with fresh spices and meat.

The next time you reach into your kitchen cupboard to grab a spice, say a prayer for the people of Pemba. There are more than 300,000 indigenous Pembans on the island; less than 0.01 percent have access to Christ.

Today, my response to serving is:

THREE MARTYRDOMS: RED, GREEN & WHITE
BY DICK BROGDEN | SUDAN

"Most assuredly, I say to you, unless a grain of wheat falls into the ground and dies, it remains alone; but if it dies, it produces much grain."

JOHN 12:24

Congratulations on making it halfway through the Live Dead challenge! Before you continue with the second half, I would like to ask you to consider dying for Jesus in three specific ways. Church history has passed down to us three essential martyrdoms. *Martyr* is a Greek word, and it simply means *witness*. The Three Martyrdoms, therefore, are three ways we can bear witness to Christ, three ways we can live dead.

THE RED MARTYRDOM

The Red Martyrdom is the most famous and the least common. We call it Red because it refers literally to dying for Jesus, to blood being spilled. The Red Martyrdom is following Jesus to physical death for your faith.

Church tradition suggests to us that the Apostle Peter moved to Rome and began to pastor the Christian community there. According to one account, persecution was so fierce that Christians began to flee the city. Peter too tried to flee Rome and the pressure, but on the way out of Rome Peter encountered Jesus. Jesus was heading against the flow, going back into the city. Surprised, Peter asked Him, *"Quo Vadis Dominae?" Where are you going, Lord?*

Jesus said, "Back into the city to die again for the flock that you desert."

Ashamed, Peter turned on his heel, returned to Rome and there witnessed in red to Jesus by being crucified upside down—upside down, according to the tradition, because he did not feel worthy to be crucified in the same manner as Christ.

Followers of Jesus through the centuries have asked the same question.

"Quo Vadis Dominae? Quo Vadis?"

Where are you going, Lord? Where are you going?

The answer of Jesus has not changed. Jesus is still going to the cross and if we are His servants, we must follow Him there. It has never been an unusual thing to die for Jesus—literally. It has happened all through history. It started with Steven and James and Paul, who in an ironic twist also witnessed in red. In the Roman Colosseum, in the Arabian Desert, in Ecuadorian jungles, in Communist jails, or islands of the Pacific—for 2,000 years men and women, old and young, have shed their blood for Jesus.

John Piper tells the story of John Patton. In the mid-1800s, a ship took two missionaries to the New Hebrides, present-day Vanuatu. The missionaries went ashore and while the crew of the boat watched, the missionaries were captured by cannibals and eaten. Twelve years later in England, Patton felt the call of God to take the gospel to the New Hebrides. An elderly gentleman in the church—I believe his name was Dixon—rebuked him: "You can't go to the New Hebrides. You'll be eaten by cannibals!"

Patton replied: "Mr. Dixon, your own prospect is soon to be laid in the grave, there to be eaten by worms. What does it matter then if you are eaten by worms and I by cannibals? For in the day of resurrection, mine will be much more glorious!"

We all die. What does it matter how? The Red Martyrdom is not to be sought, neither is it to be feared. Those who die for Christ should be considered neither heroic nor foolish. Dying for Jesus is part of the normal Christian life.

Martin Luther King Jr. said this: "We shall match your capacity to inflict suffering by our capacity to endure suffering. But be ye assured that we will wear you down by our capacity to suffer. One day we shall win freedom but not only for ourselves. We shall so appeal to your heart and conscience that we shall win you in the process, and our victory will be a double victory."

All die. Death is so normal. We have one life to live; we have one death to die.

If we can glorify Christ by Red Martyrdom, why not? It is how He died. It is where and how He went. Would it not be an honor if He allows us to go the same way? Would it not be a privilege, if in death our witness is red? If by falling to the ground and dying much fruit results, it is indeed a double victory.

THE GREEN MARTYRDOM

In about 350 A.D., a young Romanized English boy was stolen from his country. Irish pirates threw him into a leather-covered boat, bundled him across the water, and made him a slave in Ireland.

Some years later Patrick escaped and through a process of time returned to Ireland as a missionary. By this time Patrick was elderly—some think he was 72—and he gave the rest of his life to evangelize the Irish, understanding and loving them as few before or since.

By the time Patrick died, much of Ireland was Christian. Patrick and his team did such an exceptional job of preaching the gospel that Christians almost lamented that they could not die for Jesus anymore. There was little opportunity for Red Martyrdom among the fifth-century Celts.

So the Irish, being the Irish, innovated. They developed the Green Martyrdom. The Irish established missional monasteries wherever they went. These monasteries were not like the Egyptian monasteries of the Desert Fathers, who were trying to get away from the world. These monasteries were established to take the gospel to the world by interaction.

This is how it worked: Patrick and his team would go to a new location, settle in, and build houses in a ring. These houses would have a fence around them and inside the compound would be a chapel, a workshop, a dining hall, a guest lodge, and a scriptorium—a place where the monks would make copies of the Scriptures and classical literature.

These Irish were the most friendly of folk. They planted flowers and gardens, built roads and bridges, brewed ale, and shared it liberally. Their highs were high and their lows were low, and they shared life with all. A monk would station himself at the gate of the monastery and wait for travelers or guests. As soon as a traveler would come, the monk would greet him, smile, welcome him—kind of like a Wal-Mart greeter—and take the traveler right to the abbot. The abbot would welcome him again, pray for him, inquire of his news and needs, and then assign him to another monk. This monk would take him to the dining hall, feed him, find him a bed in the guesthouse, and bring the traveler to prayers. Before the guest knew what was happening, he had three new friends and had been absorbed into the life of the community. He ate their food, sang their songs, slept in their houses, shared their chores and humor, and felt immediately that he belonged.

And they did belong! This was the genius of Patrick and the Irish. This was the Celtic way of evangelism. As a team, the Irish welcomed the lost to belong before they asked for a change in belief. The Romans—and most of us today—do it the other way around. We present propositional truth and ask Muslims to agree to it, but we make no provision for community, we create no space for belonging. Hundreds of Muslims have come to Christ in Sudan, yet, sadly, very few have remained. They were rejected by one community on their profession of faith but found no new community to embrace them.

The Celtic way of evangelism put belonging ahead of believing, never sacrificing the urgency of proclamation, and in so doing Christianity spread joyously among the peoples of Ireland and Scotland.

The picture painted above sounds kind of rosy—or at least green. Why call it martyrdom? Was the Green Martyrdom, the Green Witness, all joy and celebration? No. It is called martyrdom because it still involved death—a death to self within community.

The theory of team—missionary team, body of Christ, working together—sounds wonderful. Everybody today wants to be part of community, a team, a family, and rightly so. But it does not take you very long in team or community to realize that theory and reality are two very different things. Missionary teams splinter, like Paul and Barnabas. Perhaps the greatest pain in missions is that received by the hands and tongues of friends.

If the Red Martyrdom involves laying down your life for Jesus, the Green Martyrdom requires the laying down of your will for one another. And all who have served in team among unreached people will tell you: The Green Martyrdom is so much harder.

The Live Dead initiative for church planting among unreached people is based on a team approach: four to 12 people committed to contextual ministry, long-term service in the local language, living within walking distance of each other, meeting three times a week (for prayer, for accountability, and for worship, fellowship, and teaching), and ministering together. These teams will vary in size and intensity, but one thing will never lack: the conflict of wills, opinions, and views among those who serve together.

I ask you to be a Green Martyr. I ask you to die to your opinions or views. I ask you to put your will to death.

Very few of us will be Red Martyrs. Every one of us has multiple opportunities every day to be a Green Martyr. Let's allow the Holy Spirit to reveal His control of us by how often we are willing to cede our will and way to others. Let's go Green! Let's work in teams to plant churches among unreached people.

THE WHITE MARTYRDOM

Over time, something began to gnaw at the spirits of the Green Martyrs. The monasteries were booming and blooming. Ireland is like Central Africa: everything grows. Drop your cell phone in the ground in Rwanda, and a cell phone tower will probably sprout. Life was good in Ireland, food was plentiful, and friends did abound. But something was missing.

To be content, satiated, and surrounded by friends and family was, strangely, not enough. There had to be something more in the world. There had to be higher purpose than living well, raising and educating children so they could live well, that they could do the same for their children. There had to be greater meaning in life. There had to be more than an endless cycle of prosperity.

And of course there was and there is. The Good Shepherd is not content to stay with the 99 safe if even just one is lost. The missing martyrdom was a witness of Christ to the whole world.

Columcille was a disciple of Patrick. He was commissioned to take the gospel to northern England and would do so by establishing a missional monastery at a cross-section of the sea. He would leave Ireland and sail in his leather-covered boat to the Isle of Iona.

Thomas Cahill writes: "As [Columcille] sailed off that morning, he was doing the hardest thing an Irishman could do, a much harder thing than giving up his life: He was leaving Ireland. If the Green Martyrdom had failed, here was a martyrdom that was surely equal of the Red; and henceforth, all who followed Columcille's lead were called to the White Martyrdom, they who sailed into the white sky of morning, into the unknown, never to return."

We can witness to Jesus by giving our physical lives. We must witness to Christ by following Him with surrendered wills. But there is another witness He demands of us: the White Martyrdom of taking His gospel to the ends of the earth.

In a sermon on the White Witness of Adoniram Judson, John Piper makes these remarks:

"Life is fleeting. In a very short time, we will all give an account before Jesus Christ, not only as to how well we have fulfilled our vocations, but how well we have obeyed the command to make disciples of all nations.

"Many of the peoples of the world are without any indigenous Christian movement today. Christ is not enthroned there, His grace is unknown there, and people are perishing with no access to the gospel. Most of these hopeless peoples do not want followers of Jesus to come.

"At least they think they don't. They are hostile to Christian missions. Today this is the final frontier. And the Lord still says, 'Behold, I am sending you out as sheep in the midst of wolves.' '[S]ome of you they will put to death. You will be hated by all for my name's sake. But not a hair of your head will perish' (Matthew 10:16; Luke 21:16–18).

"Are you sure that God wants you to keep doing what you are doing? For most of you, He probably does. Your calling is radical obedience for the glory of Christ right where you are. But for many of you … God wants to loosen your roots and plant you in another place.

"Some of you He is calling to fill up what is lacking in the sufferings of Christ, to fall like a grain of wheat into some distant ground and die, to hate your life in this world and so to keep it forever and bear much fruit."

Judson himself wrote to missionary candidates in 1832: "Bear in mind, that a large proportion of those who come out on a mission to the East die within five years after leaving their native land. Walk softly, therefore; death is narrowly watching your steps. The question is not whether we will die, but whether we will die in a way that bears much fruit."

God may be calling you to a Red death. That decision is in His hands. We are all called to die Green. What is desperately needed now among the unreached of the world is the White Witness whether you are red, yellow, black, or white. As you continue with the Live Dead challenge, would you daily listen to the Lord of the Harvest? He may be asking the White Martyrdom of you.

MOBILITY: A WILLING HEART
BY ROSEMARIE HANSON | KENYA

I don't deserve all that I have.

At this moment, I'm sitting in my spacious and comfortable home—a home filled with handpicked "treasures" from a variety of countries. I hear birds of all sorts chirping, cheeping, and chattering in the distance. A wind chime rings with a gentle melody as a light, cool breeze touches my cheeks. Our garden, lush and lovely, is home to all sorts of creatures—butterflies and dragonflies being my favorites.

You might think I live in some earthly version of heaven. Actually, it isn't far from the truth. I'm writing to you from Nairobi, Kenya, the place my husband and I (along with our 3-year-old daughter) live and work. In all honesty, much of Nairobi is far from paradise, but that's not the point.

For over 12 years, in spite of my beautiful surroundings, my heart was seldom at peace. For over 12 years, I couldn't quite wrap my head around the idea that I was a missionary. For over 12 years, I wrestled with God. How did I get here? Did life just "happen" to me? I didn't necessarily want to be a missionary. No burden or desire from childhood. No "call" during a powerful missions service. I was not raised in a missions-minded family. I didn't fit the mold.

But, as a high-school and university student, I wasn't interested in a white-picket-fence sort of life, either. I longed for a "different" life, one filled with travel and fascinating experiences. I just wasn't planning on a life spent in Africa. Not Africa; no thank you. Too hard. Too complicated. Too dusty. Too far. Too poor. Too rough. Too rugged. Too raw. I'm not that kind of girl.

Give me Europe. My cup of tea. Order. Beauty. Wealth. Prestige.

I was internally conflicted. I wanted my way because I believed my plans would bring me great satisfaction. On the other hand, I longed for my Creator's influence and guidance because at a more soulful level, I knew this is where a life is well lived. To fight my will, I continually looked for signs, begging God to keep my heart pure and clear, and asking for clarity regarding the future.

When I was 25, "Africa" was the answer. At 37, the answer hadn't changed. After 12 years, I couldn't seem to get rid of Africa. God kept taking me and my family back to this land. At 25, I fought (hard), I kicked (hard), I cried (hard), and I journeyed in much of my own strength. After years of hearing the same answer, I grew weary.

Several months ago while in the States, I was fighting this battle yet again. Exhausted beyond words, in desperation I met with a woman who had at one time been a missionary struggling with similar issues. In Brea, California, my entire life perspective shifted. After numerous trips back and forth across the ocean, September 2010 marked a different kind of journey. I confess I still fought (a little), kicked (a little), and cried (a little), but felt carried in strength far superior to my own.

Settling back into our home in Nairobi, I see with new eyes. The more I rest in this strength, the more my loving Creator fulfills the truest and deepest longings of my soul. The truth is, in many ways, I'm growing to love living here. We've had (and are continuing to have) productive, fulfilling, and purposeful work. We've got an incredible support system and priceless friends. We live well in Africa. After years of wrestling, my God continues to provide beautifully for us.

So here I am. Years later. Would I have liked to live the version of my life I thought I wanted? Possibly. But I've let that go. I've traded my plans, my dreams, and my aspirations. In the trading, I've learned to trust. With surrender, a goodness deeper than I thought possible has followed. The revised version of my life is much richer, sweeter, and more satisfying than the original version. I'm grateful.

My heart has ceased to be willful. My heart has become willing.

LIVE DEAD CHALLENGE

The gospel is by necessity mobile, as there are so many places and people that have not yet heard about Jesus. Is it possible that Jesus is calling you to leave all that is comfortable, all that you think completes you, in order to take the gospel where it has not yet reached? Spend 15 minutes today researching Somalia, Sudan, Comoros, Eritrea, or Djibouti.

Ask yourself, *If God asked me to move there to work with an unreached people, would my heart be willing?*

UNREACHED PEOPLE GROUP
DATOOG

Deep in the remote northern valley of Eyasi lives the Datoog tribe. The Datoog have fiercely held to their traditional lifestyle. They are nomadic pastoralists who follow the grass and rains. The ladies wear beautiful jewelry made of brass and beads, while the men have traditional scarring to emphasize their beauty.

As you go through your day, say a prayer every time you notice an unusual piece of jewelry or a tattoo. The Datoog live completely isolated from the gospel and desperately need a witness.

Today, my response to being mobile is:

Some wish to live within
the sound of a chapel bell,
I want to run a
rescue shop within
a yard of Hell. — C.T. STUDD

SCRIPTURE: THE SWORD THAT BRINGS LIFE
BY DOUG LOWENBERG | ETHIOPIA & KENYA

What does the Live Dead perspective have to do with the Bible, our guidebook and avenue for knowing God and experiencing eternal life (notice: *life*)? Isn't it interesting that the book that is written as the result of God breathing life, Spirit-life, into its authors (2 Timothy 3:16) also describes itself as a two-edged sword, living, active, piercing, doing surgery, removing the diseased and dead that life might triumph (Hebrews 4:12-13)?

The other day I wrote an e-mail to my sister to tell her about one of my creative cuisinary delights developed during a lengthy stay in a hotel where I cooked for myself to save some money. My purpose was to give information but also to attempt some humor.

I wrote: "I have been working on a new mouth-watering recipe called 'Scrambled Eggs Mexico-Micro.' I can see your eyes are widening and your stomach is getting excited! Yes, yeah verily, you take three eggs and mix thoroughly; add three packets of pepper from a local McDonald's; one and a half packets of salt from the same vendor; grab a large handful of Tostito chips and crunch them in your hands as you turn in circles singing 'Kum Ba Ya.' Add chips to egg mix and stir gently. Hit the instant button on the microwave that sets the clock for two minutes. Begin cooking and enjoy watching the eggs rise and fall like a volcano. Remove from time to time to stir and replace in micro. When the eggs are about to expand beyond the borders of your bowl (and beyond the confines of the microwave), Eggs Mexico-Micro is ready."

I copied this ridiculous message to my two grown daughters. Why? I wanted to brighten their day with my goofy humor, but more, I want them to know me, their dad, in a multifaceted way. My desire as a loving father is to communicate with them over the distance, maintaining intimate relationships by using words, sermons, advice, and counsel. I want them to know me as I report about my decisions and actions. I want them informed of my achievements and failures. I want them to know my joy, humor, and silly creativity. As they continue to grow and mature, I want them to know me in expanding horizons.

How does this relate to reading the Bible? As you plunge into God's Word, do you treat it as though you are a surgeon or scientist, anaesthetizing the patient before you begin your procedure; or as a young scientist who is dissecting a frog, you kill it before you cut it? Are you the master over the text in your analysis? Do you make the words mean what you presume they should mean?

Is this reading as one who is "dead"? Rather, how about allowing the Bible to surprise you through its familiar words? Let the Bible analyze and scrutinize you. I encourage you to read God's Word for what it is: It is God's message to you as His self-revelation. Through this book, God makes Himself present in His multifaceted nature so you can better know Him. The Bible is the medium by which we come to better understand God. As He personally talks to you, you may feel His surgical knife exposing and removing death.

You may sense His utter joy with you. You may almost audibly hear God's chuckle. He has spoken and acted in history and inspired people to write His story so you can know your Creator and Savior. The Bible exposes His thoughts and motives along with His words and deeds. As you read daily from His written revelation you are able to know God more intimately and be better prepared to surrender your destiny to Him. As Bible readers who are the living dead, you are exposed to One who also lived dead and guides you through His own example. His self-revelation reminds us: "Let this mind be in you which was also in Christ Jesus who being in the form of God … emptied himself … to the point of death" (Philippians 2:5-8).

When you open the sacred pages, hear God speak life and hope as you faithfully surrender to His two-edged sword that brings life out of death.

PRAYER

O God, surprise me today as I read Your Word.

LIVE DEAD CHALLENGE

As you did your Bible reading today, what questions did you ask about what the text is saying? What questions do you believe God, through the Word, was asking of you? What did the two-edged sword pierce?

BONI

The Boni people (also known as Aweera, Waata, or Sanye) believe they are the despised people of the earth. Their ancestors broke the bone of an animal, ate forbidden marrow, and were cast away from other people as a result. Other tribes would not intermarry with the Boni, a cursed community. About 10,000 Boni live in Kenya along the Tana River and the Indian Ocean coast. They are 99 percent Muslim, practicing folk Islam. Formerly hunters and honey gatherers, today they are moving toward agriculture.

Whenever you eat meat off a bone, pray for the Boni of Kenya. Christ was also despised (Isaiah 53:3). His bones were never broken (John 19:36), and He became cursed (Galatians 3:13) so the Boni and we could be set free from the curse and be blessed.

Today, my response to Scripture reading is:

APOSTOLIC FUNCTION: GOING WHERE JESUS IS NOT KNOWN
BY ALAN JOHNSON | THAILAND

When I walk out my door, I am surrounded by millions of people, most who are Buddhists, but also many Muslims. I walk through slums filled with the most drastic and complex of human problems. And I don't see a line of apostles, megachurch leaders, or Christian superstars waiting to get in and grapple with those realities. I don't wake up in the morning feeling apostolic. But the sheer weight of a glorious living God who loves each one of these millions He uniquely created, and the compassion of Jesus for multitudes that are harassed and helpless, compels me to respond. So I say: "Here I am, Lord. Use me to take and be your good news in this place. I will take responsibility to do what You ask me to do here."

I have come to call this response "apostolic function." People get all hung up on the word apostle, either because they want to call themselves one and take authority over others, or they don't feel like one so they sit on the sidelines waiting for someone they think is better qualified. Apostolic function is different. It means that in the face of phenomenal need, the mandate of the Bible, and the burden of the Spirit, we step up to the plate to act in an apostolic fashion to go where Jesus is not known. Whether we feel like it or not.

Our world needs literally thousands of new teams of people who will band together, like the early apostolic bands we read about in Acts, to penetrate the final ethnolinguistic groups of our world that have yet to hear and see a relevant rendering of the gospel of Jesus Christ.

If we wait until we feel apostolic, the job will never get done. Are you ready to step up to the plate and ask God to use you in this way?

We live in a world that has a shameful division: Large numbers of people have nearly unlimited potential access to the gospel via Christians, churches, and media in their sociocultural setting, while other vast blocs of humanity have either none of these, or have them in very limited number. The sad fact is that today, the vast majority of mission effort—some have estimated it at 97 percent—is misguidedly done among those who have the greatest access to the good news. It has become Christians from one place going to Christians in another place to help them, and tragically neglecting those who have no one in their culture to share and demonstrate the love of Jesus.

The crying need is for people who will step up to the plate and be willing, with God's help, to function apostolically—to commit to leading or joining a team that will focus its efforts on bringing the gospel to a people group that currently has no access.

PRAYER

- Pray that the Holy Spirit will give you courage to boldly take the gospel to the unreached.
- Begin to pray for an unreached people group. You can search online for unreached people group prayer profiles and find great resources.
- Pray that the Holy Spirit would open your eyes to neighbors who may be from places that have no gospel. You may have never seen them in this way before. Ask the Lord to guide you in connecting with them in love to share the gospel.

LIVE DEAD CHALLENGE

- To work in apostolic function means you have to travel light. Make an inventory of your life and how you spend your finances and time. What would need to change if you joined an apostolic band going to an unreached people group?
- Spend some time at www.joshuaproject.net and learn about unreached people groups in our world today.
- Talk with fellow believers about the unreached today. Now that you know about the unreached, pass that knowledge on to others and encourage them to begin praying for those who have never heard or responded in the Buddhist, Muslim, and Hindu worlds.

UNREACHED PEOPLE GROUP
ANTAISAKA

More than 1 million Antaisaka people live in the southeastern rain forest of Madagascar near the town of Vangiandrano. They are the most unreached tribe in Madagascar, mainly because poor roads and trails make access to their region difficult.

These animistic people cultivate coffee, bananas, and, like most Malagasy people, rice. They are governed by strong taboos, which hold the people in bondage. Many Antaisaka homes have a separate door in the back of the house to remove the bodies of those who have died. As with all Malagasies, the dead hold a strong place in the people's lives. The Antaisaka bury their dead in a communal burial house called a *kibory*. The corpses, wrapped like mummies, are prepared and then left to dry out for two or three years before they are finally placed in the burial house.

The next time you see a mummy on television or in a magazine, please pray for the Antaisaka people.

Today, my response to apostolic function is:

PROCLAMATION: DO NOT BE SILENCED
BY STEVE OVERTURF | SUDAN

When the people heard this, they were cut to the heart and said to Peter and the other apostles, "Brothers, what shall we do?" Peter replied, "Repent and be baptized, every one of you, in the name of Jesus Christ for the forgiveness of your sins." ... With many other words he warned them; and he pleaded with them.

ACTS 2:37-38, 40

Day after day, in the temple courts and from house to house, they never stopped teaching and proclaiming the good news that Jesus is the Christ.

ACTS 5:42

"No problem. All religions are one!" my Muslim acquaintance said when I told him I followed Jesus. Had I came to this Muslim nation only to encounter more of the same relativism I thought I'd left behind? I considered my response, as others were involved in the conversation. This is a culture of shame, where embarrassment is to be avoided at all costs. I wondered if I should minimize my response in hopes of another opportunity later on. I wondered if I should be subtle and if my relationship with him had reached the level of trust needed to sustain a frank response. Perhaps I should check the barometric pressure and wind patterns while I'm at it!

We've done so much rationalization regarding how and when we proclaim the gospel that we have a hundred reasons why we don't. There's much we can say about how not to do it, but let us never fail to be people of action. We will always be learning how to proclaim, but without fire in our bones we will get nowhere. The gospel means "news," and good news at that. Let's not treat it as a mere philosophy, way of life, discussion fodder, or means of self-help.

We have urgent news to proclaim: "Danger! Our sin condemns us before the Holy Creator who demands a payment for our rebellion. Our insurrection will be punished! But wait ... there is a way! He's provided an escape! God's Son Himself has broken through enemy lines to lead us out! Quickly, come!"

My gospel summary has a lot of exclamation points. Our proclamation of the gospel must bear such marks of passion.

Evangelism can be uncomfortable, even scary. Take heart; you're not alone. The Holy Spirit came to help us in this. If you're not scared sometimes, check your pulse. If you love Jesus, it's in your DNA to share the reason for the hope you have. Perhaps you've felt pressured to evangelize in the past and have resented it. Understandable, but let us forgive any heavy-handedness we may have experienced and hear again the call of Jesus to make disciples.

The greatest good we can ultimately do is to point people toward their one hope in Jesus. If we've met their physical, social, educational, or emotional needs without doing something to tell them of the forgiveness found in Jesus, we have not eternally helped. Let our words and actions both cry out, "Turn to Jesus!" Our Christlike integrity or good deeds do not point clearly enough to Jesus if we don't proclaim the gospel out loud. The world may have grown tired of religious talk, but the gospel is still "the power of God for the salvation for everyone who believes." Yet "how can they hear without someone preaching to them?" Don't be silenced! Verbal proclamation is still central to God's plan.

When we are full of God's Spirit and Word, normal conversations become opportunities for sowing seeds. Can you prayerfully consider how you might interject Jesus or the Bible into your greetings or casual conversation? Let us allow the Spirit to help us be creative in witness even as we glean from others.

I answered my Muslim friend with a smile, saying: "Well, you and I are the same in that we are both guilty before God. But only Jesus can take away your shame and mine. Jesus came as much for you as He did for me. Put your trust in Him and He'll bring you to paradise." There's life in the truth of those words!

LIVE DEAD CHALLENGE

- Roland Allen wrote a great book, *Missionary Methods: St. Paul's or Ours?* Get your hands on it if you can. If not, study the ministry of the Apostles in Acts (2:14-41, 3:12-26, 4:8-12, 5:17-32, 8:4-8, 8:26-34, 10:34-43, 13:14-41, 16:13-15). Look for the centrality of proclamation in the life of every New Testament figure. What is the implication for you?

- Have you sought the Holy Spirit for power in your proclamation?
- Pray for an opportunity to proclaim this week what God has done through Jesus. Hold yourself accountable with another believer and share your reports.

ANTANKARANA

The Antankarana people number nearly 300,000 and live in the far northeastern tip of Madagascar. Their name means *people of the rocks* because of the many jagged outcroppings of rock found in that part of the country. These isolated people are Islamic in their faith, dating back to early interaction with Arab traders in the 1700s and 1800s. Their Islamic faith is mainly cultural, and many villages have no organized mosque, Koran, or even basic religious training.

Antankarana people are often fishermen, and they have strong taboos that govern everyday life. Houses are usually built on stilts above the ground. Amber Mountain is the largest mountain in that region and is known for its rugged national park.

The next time you are driving and a stoplight turns amber, stop your car and pray for the Antankarana people until the light turns green.

Today, my response to proclamation is:

SUFFERING: DO YOU KNOW HIM ENOUGH TO TRUST HIM?
BY CHRISTI JONES | JORDAN

And we know that in all things God works for the good of those who love him, who have been called according to his purpose.

ROMANS 8:28

As Christians, we know this Scripture. We quote it often. We love it when good times are coming our way, and we can accept a difficult circumstance when we see how God might redeem it and use it. However, there are some things in life that happen that seem to contradict our theology; things that happen that make it seem as though God is no longer in control; things like suffering.

Suffering comes in all forms, and the entire human race is subject to it—but we don't like it. When the government officials came to our office and kicked us out and sealed the door; when we were threatened with expulsion from the land of our calling; when we wondered what our future held—we suffered some emotional trauma. But we knew that God was good and that He would work it out. We could trust Him with the outcome.

However, on the morning of February 3, 2000, when I heard my husband's frantic voice say, "Layla's not breathing," everything in my life turned upside down. Our 1-year-old daughter had been fighting a virus for a couple of days, and I had been up two nights with her. The lack of sleep over the previous 48 hours added to my difficulty to understand what was happening as my husband began CPR. *This can't be real!* Panic gripped me. I ran to the phone and called two Jordanian friends and asked them to pray as I screamed out, "Layla's gone." Our 10-year-old daughter, awakened by the screaming and commotion, ran to ask help from our neighbors. I prayed as my body shook with the shock and with a fear that overtook my entire being.

The days, weeks, and months that followed Layla's death were the darkest days of my life. The only sleep offered to me was filled with nightmares. The enemy of my soul came to accuse and confuse me: "What kind of mother are you to let your child die?" "Where was your God when your daughter was dying?" "If you weren't a missionary, this wouldn't have happened!" "God must hate you to do this to you!" "What sin have you committed that God would do this to you?" "You, a missionary? Hah! You don't even trust God, do you? Look what He did to you?" The darkness that filled my heart and mind at times was terrifying. My words cannot describe it fully.

My husband, broken as he was, kept saying, "God is good." Was He? Yes. I had believed that before February 3. But what about now? What about in the midst of all that was happening? As I stumbled through each day after the funeral, I couldn't even pray. Surrounded by my family who had traveled to Jordan to be with us and by our Jordanian friends, I felt so completely alone. My heart was breaking. The guilt of not somehow saving my daughter, the grief of not having her, was overwhelming me. I couldn't go on. Was God good? If He had been before February 3, wasn't He the same now? He never changes. I had believed that. But now my situation was different. What about now?

Through the darkness, fear, and loneliness that had become my life, God in His mercy reached out and held me in a way I never experienced before or since. God brought back to my memory a vision regarding Jordan He had given me five years before, and I felt it was a promise of His spiritual refreshing that would come. People around us speculated whether we would leave our calling, but God in His gentle way had given me that vision five years previously to be a point of hope for the future when I needed it. As I thought over my life, I knew that God had been so faithful, so good, and though my attempts were so feeble at first, I reaffirmed my trust in Him and in His goodness.

The loss of a child is considered to be one of the greatest of all emotional pains. There were many days when getting out of bed occurred only because my 8-year-old and 10-year-old needed food or help to prepare for school. Each day I asked for God's help to survive the day, and I found that each day He gave me the ability. One day one daughter asked if I would ever smile again, and I assured her I would. At the time, though, I didn't really believe what I was saying. But God knew. He knew He was able to turn mourning into dancing if we just held on to Him. Suffering is never without purpose. God takes it all—the pain, the tears, the fear, the confusion, the questions, the doubts—and uses it to build us up in our faith, to help us see who He is, if we trust Him through it all. For years I had sung the song "All to Jesus I surrender, All to Him I freely give. I will ever love and trust Him, in His presence daily live." Was that true? Would I? Even though I didn't understand all that was happening in my life, I knew God would help me if I wouldn't run from Him. I wanted to finish what He had called me to do and to be, even if it hurt. He would be and has been faithful.

So then, those who suffer according to God's will should commit themselves to their faithful Creator and continue to do good.

1 PETER 4:19

Our griefs cannot mar the melody of our praise; they are simply the bass notes of our life song: "To God Be the Glory."

C. H. SPURGEON

LIVE DEAD CHALLENGE

List three people whose death would profoundly affect you. Now, go before the Lord in prayer about how you would react if each of those people died. What would it affect? What would it change? Do you know Him enough to know you can trust Him, even with the pain of life? Would you continue to obey Him no matter the cost? Do you trust in His goodness? Will you share in His sufferings?

SOMALI (SOUTHERN SOMALIA)

We first met Mohamed when he was 5 years old. He was a normal, active boy, full of investigative mischief and sharp as a tack. He had a strange round scar in the middle of his forehead, and other similar scars encircled his head. Eventually our curiosity led us to investigate the origin of these marks. We learned that when Mohamed was a baby, his parents decided that his head was too big for his body. A lit cigarette was used to mark a boundary around his head in an attempt to keep it from getting any bigger.

In rural Somalia, where modern medical care is largely unavailable, burning is commonly used as a cure for "whatever ails you." A thin metal rod is heated in a fire and used to burn a series of small scars over the affected area—your stomach, an arm, a leg.

Whenever you see the flame of a match, a candle, a campfire, or the glow of a lit cigarette, remember the many Somalis who bear the scars of "traditional healing methods." Pray that Jesus, the True Light, would shine truth into their ignorance and bring healing to their bodies.

Today, my response to suffering is:

The blood of
the martyrs
is always the
seed of
the church.

I have but one candle of life to burn, and I would rather

burn it out in a land filled with darkness than a land flooded with light.

– JOHN KEITH FALCONER

WORSHIP: TIME IN HIS PRESENCE
BY HELEN NEST | SUDAN

Then the king said to Araunah, "No, but I will surely buy it from you for a price; not will I offer burnt offerings to the Lord my God with that which costs me nothing."

2 SAMUEL 24:24

Sometimes when I put my children in bed at night, I stand in the darkness of their shared room and begin to worship the Lord. I lift my voice and my hands in praise, and often my children join me. Lying in bed, they lift their hands and hearts in worship, and frequently fall asleep praising the Lord. No matter who we are, what we have or don't have, we can always give Him praise. Some praise costs more than others, and costly praise is especially beautiful to Jesus.

Our daughter had expressed some interest in going to boarding school so that she could play soccer with other girls her age. She didn't want to leave us, but at the same time wanted to experience all that the school had to offer. The school she was attending would cease to offer education after the eighth grade. Ninth grade was creeping up on us and spinning my heart into a panic. We had asked her months before to make it a matter of prayer.

I plugged in the iPod at the kitchen table and kicked off my shoes. I knew the only place I could find peace over this matter was in His presence. I began to pace back and forth, trying to fix my eyes on Jesus, nothing of my troubles, nothing of my plans, just on the sweetness and beauty of who He is: the Lion of Judah, the soon and coming King, my Shepherd, my Deliverer, my Comfort. Flashes of memories came pouring through my mind of the ways in which He had delivered me, rescued me, and redeemed me in times past. Out of this my heart began to swell and tears began to spill from my eyes. "O Jesus, You are my faithful one, no one is trustworthy like You, You know all and see all, my life is in Your hands." The worship passed from the solitude of my mind to my lips.

At this point a song rang from the iPod that I believe the Lord put there just for me that day: "I'm pouring out my praise on you; I'm pouring out my love on you."

Fixated in my mind was a picture of Mary sitting at the feet of Jesus, pouring her precious perfume on His feet. In His presence I found myself desperate for an offering to give Him. The realization of His majesty was so capturing my heart, and I felt empty-handed in front of a king. At that moment an image of my daughter flashed before my eyes. Could I give her to Him? Could I lay the whole idea of boarding school at His feet and even know that He would have her go and be obedient to it?

The worship leader on my iPod then spoke out, "If you are still measuring out your offerings, you haven't seen His worth."

As Mary poured out her perfume, so I began to pour out Larissa onto His feet. "You are worth it, Jesus. You are worth living in this hot desert that is filled with oppression. You are worth giving up comfort and convenience to bring truth to the unreached. You are even worth allowing my daughter to go to boarding school." Peace flooded me, my heart, my nerves … they were all still, silenced in the majesty of God. And then He flooded my heart with His love.

It's amazing what time in His presence can do. It can wash you clean, set you free, even allow the chance for your child to experience boarding school. That afternoon at home, I was preparing dinner when my daughter walked into the kitchen. She had no idea why I had taken time away with Jesus that day. As she likes to do, she just kind of hung by my side while I chopped veggies. She then said: "Mom, Jesus spoke to me today. He told me that it was okay for me to go to boarding school next year." How my God gently leads us. What a faithful God have I!

LIVE DEAD CHALLENGE

What names or characteristics of God stand out to you? Think over how He has delivered you and redeemed you in times past. Was He a shelter for you? Was He a gentle shepherd leading you? You have your own unique circumstances in the story of your life where He has shown Himself to you. Express verbally who He is and who He has been to you.

Is there an offering that you are still holding back and measuring out? Find a place to secretly meet with Him; catch a glimpse of His majesty. See what your offering looks like then. Give Jesus something costly today as an act of worship.

UNREACHED PEOPLE GROUP

NDZWANI

The Ndzwani people are blessed to live on the most beautiful of the four Comorian islands, Anjouan. The island is teeming with life and beauty. Waterfalls, mountains, forests, rivers, and beaches make Anjouan an aesthetically pleasing place to live. Yet in the midst of all the natural beauty and life are about 300,000 Ndzwani people who are spiritually dead. The Ndzwani are a Muslim people who mix traditional Islam with spirit worship. They desperately need the breath of life breathed into their families, communities, cultures, and souls.

The next time you see something beautiful in nature that grabs your attention, turn your thoughts to the Ndzwani people and pray that God would infuse these islanders with a life full of hope, peace, joy, and faith.

Today, my response to worshipping God is:

FLEXIBILITY: GOD'S MUSIC, WRITTEN IN THREE FLATS

BY BOB MCCULLEY | TANZANIA, KENYA, RWANDA & SUDAN

Some of the most dangerous times in our life and ministry are when we lock our dreams and hopes in concrete, when we become so focused on what we are planning to do that we cannot see what God is trying to do. One day while serving among the Maasai people of East Africa, I was running late for an appointment to meet with the village elders in a place called Mbirikani, which was about an hour away from our home. The purpose of the meeting was to appeal for a site where we could build a church in that village. My planned departure was delayed and my wife, Murriell, tried to soothe my anxiety with the words, "God has everything under control."

I drove my four-by-four station wagon quickly up the road and was making good time until I got a flat tire, which I hurriedly changed. A few miles later, I had a second flat and again made a tire change that would make a pit crew proud. Deep in the bush and well off the road, I had a third flat tire, and my third and final spare had to be removed from the luggage rack. In the process of getting it off the roof, it rolled away from me and down the hill into a large clump of thorn brush. By the time I retrieved it, my clothes were torn and my face and arms were bleeding from multiple scratches.

As I was preparing to mount the third spare tire, a Morani, a Maasai warrior, came walking out of the forest and greeted me. I did not wish to have a conversation because I was dirty from changing the flats and was now very late for what I thought was a critical appointment. His greeting was congenial and correct, while mine was harsh and abrupt. But I had good reason: I was late, dirty, bleeding, and angry. His next words stopped me. He knew my name. He had heard me preach a few weeks before, and that morning on awakening had decided to go to town to find me and to ask me to help him receive Christ. He had set off before sunrise to walk about 15 miles to town to find me and only halfway there, had found me on the roadside. I stopped changing the tire, cleaned my hands, and got my Bible out. Soon we were sitting under a thorn tree, reading and praying together as he became a newborn follower of Jesus.

When we were done, he thanked me and disappeared back into the forest, and I sat in wonder of the way God schedules our lives. By then I knew I had been right on time for the only appointment God had scheduled for me that day. I had no spare tires left, so I finished mounting the third spare and turned the truck around and headed home. Days later, I learned that the meeting had been postponed until the following day and our appeal had been granted. The community had given us 10 acres of ground on which to develop the ministry.

Our plans and dreams are often far removed from what God has in mind for us, and a lack of flexibility may cause us to miss Him and to be broken in the missing.

LIVE DEAD CHALLENGE

Look for a way you can be flexible today. Anticipate an interruption and welcome it as an opportunity, an event God has scheduled for you—even if it makes you late or it means that something you planned does not happen. In the days to come, look for ways you can be flexible. In service opportunities down the road, commit to flexing—dying to your plan and schedule that you might live to the surprises God injects in your daily life.

OROMO

Oromo means *the powerful*.
The Oromo are an ethnic
group found in Ethiopia,
northern Kenya, and to
a lesser extent in parts of
Somalia. With 30 million
members, they constitute the
single largest ethnic group

in Ethiopia and about 34 percent of the population, according
to the 2007 census. At the time of the last census, 47.5 percent
were Muslims, 30.5 percent Orthodox Christians, and 17.7
percent Protestant Christian.

About 95 percent are settled agriculturalists and nomadic
pastoralists, "practicing" archaic farming methods and living at
subsistence level. A few live in the urban centers. The Oromo
are divided into two major branches that break down into an
assortment of clan families.

**Please pray for the Oromo. Pray that they will become
a missionary people. Pray that Oromo men and women
will be saved, filled with the Holy Spirit, and sent as
missionaries to their Somali neighbors. Every time
you hear about Ethiopia, would you pray for hundreds
of missionaries to be sent from Ethiopia to Muslim
peoples.**

Today, my response to being flexible is:

HOSPITALITY: OUR FAITH IN ACTION
BY NATALIE OVERTURF | SUDAN

There is a knock at my door and my heart sinks. I anticipate who stands on the other side. It is a neighbor who knows that I am home. She loves to spend time together, although the language barrier is so great we can barely communicate. I feel like a prisoner in my own home! She knows I am home, so choosing not to answer my door is to risk offending her.

I go to the door. Suspicions are confirmed and I invite her inside. I smile outwardly and grumble inwardly. At this point I am new on the field and a young mom with two toddlers. I enjoy spending time with this neighbor, but she always seems to knock at the most inconvenient moment—and this day is no exception. I offer her a seat in my living room as I go to the kitchen to prepare something to drink. Alone in my kitchen, I throw my hands in the air and "scream" in a whisper, "I don't even want you to be here!"

Alone in my kitchen? I might as well have spoken those words in front of an audience of thousands. More sobering is that I had just spoken those words in front of Jesus Christ Himself. Just months earlier I had stood before churches that sent me overseas for opportunities like this very one—and yet here I was in my kitchen, resentful of the "imposition." God forbid that I ever see a human soul as an imposition.

God's grace covered that incident and yet, years later, there are still times when my heart can sink over a knock at the door. At those moments I continue to learn to put myself aside and my agenda aside, and His heart grows in me more and more.

Something unique happens when we serve in our homes, something that cannot be replicated in other places. Whether it is ministering within our own family, the greater Body of Christ, or to unbelievers, I believe that *our home is one of the most powerful arenas to affect a life for God.*

Hospitality is our faith in action. It is prayerfully preparing a meal, inviting the Holy Spirit to lead and bless the conversation and fellowship. It is giving and often sacrificing time and focused attention to those whom Christ brings into our homes and seeing each one as Jesus does—because hospitality is really all about the way we see people.

When I get in the way, I find myself trying to impress and grumbling at the inconvenience of hospitality. It is often far from glamorous, and much of the work is done behind the scenes. There are no accolades for serving someone a meal or providing rest and refuge. There are times when God asks us to serve in a way that allows for others to be effective in their more outward and applauded roles; but this service is precious in God's sight. It comes down to obedience.

We are told in Scripture (Romans 12:13) to practice hospitality. Hospitality also defined the lives of leaders in Scripture (1 Timothy 3:2, Titus 1:8). To not seek to grow in the practice and grace of hospitality would be nothing less than disobedience.

Hospitality isn't about me. It is rarely, if ever, convenient. It isn't about appearances. It has everything to do with the way we see and receive people, in our homes and wherever we are. It is Jesus' heart alive in us extending an invitation to all who will come. It is the attitude of my heart about the value of the human soul that causes me to reach out and draw others in, inviting them into our homes and lives. Come, live out the kingdom by learning to lavishly love and serve.

LIVE DEAD CHALLENGE

So often when we think of living a life of surrender to Jesus, we tend to focus on the "big." This is where we paint with broad strokes on the canvas of our lives with prayers such as, "Jesus, I will go anywhere and do anything ..." These altars where we commit our lives to God in this way are critical. However, when we find ourselves having gone to that place called "anywhere" and we are living out what often seem to be mundane tasks, we must regard these as holy before the Lord. It is here where all the details of Christ's character being formed in us are put upon the canvas in much smaller strokes. If we are not careful, we can find ourselves busily trying to paint a beautiful picture *for* God instead of aligning ourselves with the Spirit and allowing Him to take the brush and have His way.

As you reflect on the following questions, prayerfully consider how God is speaking to you about where He wants to be most comfortable: your heart.

- Do I find that I am inconvenienced by unexpected things that come my way, or do I see them as something God may be orchestrating and seek to join Him in what He is doing?
- Do I see my home as a powerful place to affect a life for God?
- What is the attitude of my heart in regard to the value of people?
- Am I impatient with the "smallness" of serving?

This week, invite someone you would not normally invite to your house for a home-cooked meal. Lavish love on your guests and end the fellowship by praying with them and for them.

UNREACHED PEOPLE GROUP
BARA

The Bara people are a highly animistic tribe in south-central Madagascar. They number more than 800,000 and in many ways live a Wild West-type existence. They pride themselves in raising large herds of cattle—and also pride themselves in being the island's best cattle thieves. Training is offered in Bara towns on how to most effectively steal cattle and get away with it.

Women play an inferior role in Bara culture, but men gain status by stealing cattle, fighting fiercely, or by killing an enemy. The Bara fear spirits and ghosts and bury their dead in high caves on the sides of cliffs.

The next time you pass a herd of cattle, pray for the Bara people, that God would free them from the violent and twisted culture in which they live.

Today, my response to hospitality is:

GIVING: INVESTING IN ETERNITY
BY JOHN H. MORTON | SUDAN

I stared at the red Corvette in the lane next to me and heard, *That could be yours, you know.* Clearly, I heard a voice, a voice that was directed to my soul. The light turned green, and I stepped on the accelerator. I tried to shake the thoughts rushing through my brain, but I couldn't. *That could be yours* played over and over again.

What if I didn't go into full-time ministry? Is that so bad? I could become a businessman, make lots of money, and even drive a Corvette—but of course give generously to the church. Suddenly, I snapped back to reality. Whoa. Where did that come from? I knew the Lord had directed me to study to become a full-time minister. Financial sacrifices were sure to come with the territory, but did I really want to sacrifice?

I knew I was at a crossroad, one that I thought I would never be at again. Not true. I finished my studies and became an ordained minister. I worked for several years as a music pastor, enjoying life but collecting few material goods along the way. And amazingly, I didn't mind. In fact, even though my wife and I didn't have much, we found we thoroughly enjoyed giving—giving time, giving hospitality, giving money.

The Lord always took care of us. One day, before our two daughters were old enough for school, my wife took them to McDonald's for lunch. Money was tight, and my wife realized that she had only enough change for one hamburger and one drink. She purchased the food and sat down, holding their little pudgy hands and thanking the Lord. When they raised their heads, a manager came around the corner. She looked at them and said, "Did y'all order a hamburger?" My wife explained that she already had the one she ordered. "Well," the manager responded, "I don't know what happened, but this one here is extra, so you might as well eat it."

My wife told me later that God did a miracle that moment in McDonald's. Was the hamburger such a big deal? Not really, but God's detailed care of her life spoke volumes.

That lesson repeated itself through the years as we began using more and more of our income for what I call eternal investments. We almost became giddy when we had enough money to add "one more missionary" to our giving list or help a friend with groceries.

Ironically, the Lord opened the door for us to become business owners. We understood that this was the right step for us this time because the Lord knew He could trust us with His resources. Yes, we could now afford a Corvette. But living dead means dying to the immediate (leather interior and ragtop roof) and living for the eternal (fully loaded crown).

We thought that our series of "crossroads" had ended. Not so. The Lord had one more act of giving to ask of us. He asked us to give up the well-established, much-respected life we knew to go to a hot, dusty land with few roads and even fewer Corvettes. He asked us to give our lives to tell Muslims about the greatest act of giving—Jesus.

In Matthew 19:29, Jesus says, "And everyone who has left houses or brothers or sisters or father or mother or children or fields for my sake will receive a hundred times as much and will inherit eternal life."

To an investor, "a hundred times" is a return beyond his wildest dreams. Who wouldn't want to invest in a "sure thing"? Well, lots of people. Why? Because living-dead giving hurts. You have to die to your wants, die to a society that tells you what you need, die to that three-bedroom house with the white picket fence, die to that amazing new car on the showroom floor. Ouch.

Living dead requires a heart that gives more than a tithe, more than an obligatory offering. Living dead asks you to give quickly and freely. Matthew 10:8a says, "You have freely received; freely give."

LIVE DEAD CHALLENGE

Are you ready to give? Begin by being honest. Ask yourself: Do I tithe? Am I even doing the basics? Tithing is a no-brainer. If you are a follower of Jesus, you are to invest a portion of your income to the church where you are planted. That's just the beginning, but once you understand the principle of giving you realize that it is impossible to out-give God. If you truly trust in His care for you, you'll release your resources knowing that He will continue to provide.

Maybe you think, *I don't have much money, but when I get a real job, when I hit it big … watch out!* That's flawed thinking. In the Gospels, a small boy offered his five loaves of bread and two fish to Jesus. Not much when considering the thousands of people present. Yet when given to Jesus, the small amount met the need with 12 baskets left over. The boy could have thought, *But this is all I have. If I give this, I won't have enough for me. How will I survive?*

Malachi 3 says: "Bring your full tithe to the Temple treasury so there will be ample provisions. … Test me in this and see if I don't open up heaven itself to you and pour out blessings beyond your wildest dreams."

The Lord says, "Test me." In other words, practice giving. Start by being faithful in tithing. For another challenge, forget the daily latte and put a $20 bill in your pocket. Ask the Lord to direct your steps in giving it away today. Maybe it's helping a single mom with car repairs, a missionary trying to get to the field, an elderly man with an overdue utility bill. Be open. Challenge yourself to continually increase your giving, and as you do journal God's provision in your life.

HARARI

The Harari people are known as
the only ethnic group in Ethiopia
affiliated entirely with one religion,
Sunni Islam. The Harari speak Gey
Sinan. With the Egyptian conquest
of the city of Harar, numerous words
have been "taken" from the Arabic
language. Gey Sinan was originally
written in Arabic and more recently
converted into the Ge'ez alphabet.
Most Harari people are bilingual in
Amharic and Oromo.

Composing just under 10 percent within their own city, Harari
people have moved throughout Ethiopia, mainly to Addis
Ababa and Dire Dawa, establishing families and businesses. The
Harari people have also spread throughout North America as
well, mainly living in cities such as Washington, D.C., Atlanta,
and Toronto.

**Whenever you take a long trip away from home, pray
for the Harari people. They are considered by some
to be the least-reached people in Ethiopia. Pray they
would find their way to an eternal home.**

Today, my response to giving is:

The command has been to 'go,' but we have stayed — in body, gifts, prayer and influence. He has asked us to be witnesses unto the uttermost parts of the earth. But 99% of Christians have kept puttering around in the homeland. — ROBERT SAVAGE

HUMILITY: VALUING OTHERS ABOVE YOURSELF
BY RIVER THOMPSON | SUDAN

Do nothing out of selfish ambition or vain conceit. Rather, in humility value others above yourselves, not looking to your own interests but each of you to the interests of the others.

PHILIPPIANS 2:3

Thirty years ago, I started my college teaching career. After many initial bumps and bruises in the classroom, caused by my lack of experience and a fear of public speaking, I found out that being a college professor was quite fulfilling. But the fulfillment came in two forms: the genuine pleasure of helping others grow in their knowledge and the artificial high one received in being looked up to and being called by titles. After all, *doctor* sounds so much more impressive than *mister.*

In my case, those early years of college teaching coincided with the early years of my Christian walk. I was voraciously reading the Bible. Principles were being formed within me, oftentimes without much recognition or any special effort on my part.

One such principle was that of humility. I saw it lived out in Jesus as I read through the Scriptures. But I recognized the antithesis of humility on the college campus and within me. It sure was nice to be on that pedestal. In reality, however, I was a lightweight on campus. Some of the other faculty members had developed arrogance and preening to an art form. It was like being at a bodybuilding contest, but the muscles that were greased and on display were human brains.

As is often the case, we fail to see in ourselves what we dislike seeing in others. In comparing myself to others, I did not look so bad. It was those other egotistical professors that should be humbled by the Lord. However, the sin in me was what interested the Lord.

So what does it mean to be humble in the biblical sense? We need look no further than the characteristics of Jesus. He had every right to see Himself as special, privileged, and worthy of honor. But instead, He displayed a deferential attitude and became subservient to those He sought to seek and to save. Should I not emulate Him in those very characteristics? Had my recent salvation experience taught me nothing? Through it, did I not recognize that my knowledge, influence, and power were very limited? Doesn't the Bible urge us to humble ourselves and pray (2 Chronicles 7:14)? Does it not warn us that "whoever exalts himself will be humbled" (Matthew 23:12)?

These truths began to grow in me as my teaching career continued. God gave me a genuine love and respect for my students. Their interests, primarily a desire to learn, became my interests. The Bible exhorted me to value others above myself (Philippians 2:3). But humility is not a constant companion. Pride and arrogance are ever-present enemies waiting to pounce. My sin nature is always ready to receive praise and adoration, and it rebels against humility and servanthood.

My lessons in humility (and other godly characteristics) continued for nearly three decades. It was only then that the Lord decided to call me into missionary service. What a privilege it is, but additional humility is required. Just as Jesus was sent by the Father to seek and to save, I am being sent by the Son to serve and to share. The impact of the gospel message is severely blunted when it is not offered in a spirit of love, grace, and humility. Jesus Himself promised, "… those who humble themselves will be exalted" (Luke 14:11). Nothing makes a follower of Jesus feel more exalted than to lead someone to Christ, to disciple a new believer, to see a church launched, or, in short, to see the unreached reached.

LIVE DEAD CHALLENGE

A Turkish believer who spoke at the Third Lausanne Congress on World Evangelization said that he judges missionaries by a "humility index." If they are humble, he prays that they stay and are used mightily. If they are not humble, he prays God takes them away from Turkey, to trouble their own people back home. See if you can make it for a week without referencing yourself, or anything you have done, both in conversation or writing.

Editor's note: Dr. River Thompson was the chairman of the engineering department at a prestigious U.S. university, making a six-figure salary. He walked away from the prestige and power to serve simply in Sudan, arriving with no job and no title.

ETHIOPIAN AFAR

Afar land is mainly rocky and desert terrain. Afar people live in the Awash Valley of Ethiopia, the rocky hills of northern Djibouti, and the arid coastland of southern Eritrea.

In the Ethiopian Afar areas, there are only two hospitals available to the Afar, and the Afar people in this area are usually found to be malnourished. Their diets consist mainly of bread and milk. There is no natural source of water for the Afar people. Water must be tanked in, and as a result it is relatively expensive. Many of the Afar people have anemia and malaria because of their inadequate diets.

The Afar are 99 percent Muslim with a few dozen believers in Ethiopia. **Every time you drink a glass of milk, use milk while cooking, or add milk to a hot drink, would you remember to pray for the Afar. Pray that the blood of Jesus shed on the cross for the Afar will not have been spilled in vain.**

Today, my response to humility is:

FOLLOWERSHIP: SUBMITTING TO AUTHORITY
BY PAM MORTON | SUDAN

"Follow me," Jesus said. Peter looked at Jesus' gaze and paused. He had a decision to make. If he followed Jesus, he would leave what he knew. Familiar routines, skills, expectations, friendships would all change. If he stayed, he would never know where Jesus would lead him.

Follow me.

In this context, following doesn't seem so bad. Who wouldn't want to follow Jesus if He issued a personal invitation? But being a follower of Christ also means following those He puts in authority over us, and let's be honest—they are not Jesus, at least not in the way we expect.

Mary Slessor, a single missionary to the jungles of Nigeria in the 1800s, asked permission to marry a fellow worker from another station. Her superiors denied her request, stating that both workers were needed in their respective areas. Mary accepted their decision and continued in her work for the rest of her life alone. Unfair? But didn't they understand how lonely she was? How dangerous it could be for a female?

As a result of her years of labor, a tribe of cannibals stopped eating their visitors, no longer killed twin babies, became believers in Jesus, and elevated her to the level of magistrate within their community.

Like Peter, she had a choice. "Follow me," Jesus said. Follow me into dark, insect-infested jungles. Follow me to people who proudly invoke the very powers of hell. Follow me when decisions are made that you don't understand. Follow me when leaders are imperfect, sometimes cranky and inconsistent, but also demonstrate my grace and mercy in their lives. Follow me when I ask you to submit to authority as I submitted to the cross.

Paul said, "Follow me as I follow Christ." He also said, "You reap what you sow." Sow good following and you will reap good followers. Good followers actually lead other followers by example from a submitted heart and an understanding that all authority comes from God.

Romans 13:1-2 declares: "Everyone must submit himself to the governing authorities, for there is no authority except that which God has established. The authorities that exist have been established by God. Consequently, he who rebels against the authority is rebelling against what God has instituted, and those who do so will bring judgment on themselves."

C. T. Studd attended Cambridge University, becoming a school legend by his ability in cricket. Soon he and his fellow teammates were hailed all throughout England as heroes. Studd heard Jesus say, "Follow me." He left the accolades of adoring sports fans, speaking engagements, box seats, invitation-only parties, and lucrative endorsements and went to China, India, and Africa to establish a front line for the gospel. He said, "Some want to live within the sound of church or chapel bell; I want to run a rescue shop within a yard of hell."

His life demonstrated that Studd sometimes followed well and at other times did not. Isn't that the story for all of us? We become frustrated, annoyed, and even angry when following doesn't turn out like we had hoped. Grandiose ideas along the lines of "Well, if I were leading …" or "If only he would …" begin to form and soon following become a waiting pattern for usurping. Jesus never said, "Usurp power." He said, "Follow me." Did He know how fallible His church leaders would be? Yes, all too well. But He also knew that the power of the Holy Spirit would provide everything necessary to live well, lead well, and follow well. Our responsibility is to allow time in our day to receive the equipping.

Follow me.

LIVE DEAD CHALLENGE

I suspect most leaders know when their followers are unhappy, but have they heard from those followers who are committed to serving, loving, and extending grace? This week write down the names of those who are in authority over you. Plan a time to call, write, or meet them. Affirm in your conversation that you appreciate their leadership, are committed to helping them, and will be loyal in spirit and deed. Pray for them daily and ask the Lord to give you a heart that follows well.

UGANDAN NUBIANS

During the engagement process, a Nubian bride may require a car, a house, or promise of monogamy from her prospective groom. Cigarettes are commonly included in the dowry given to the bride's family, and the bride's first duty after the marriage ceremony is to cook a meal that is evaluated by the groom's family.

The Nubians are the one tribe in Uganda that is nearly 100 percent Islamic.

Nubian men are remembered for their infamous role as leaders and solders in Idi Amin's army, and the women are more admirably noted for their skillful weaving. **Whenever you see a woven basket, pray for the Nubians of Uganda.**

Centuries ago the forefathers of the Nubians were followers of Christ. Tragically, this is now true of less than 1 percent of the 15,000 Nubians living in Uganda.

Today, my response to following authority is:

.

TEAM: FRUITFULNESS THROUGH DIVERSITY
BY CLYDELL HEUGEL | KENYA, TANZANIA & SUDAN

There are diversities of gifts, but the same Spirit. There are differences of ministries, but the same Lord. And there are diversities of activities, but it is the same God who works all in all.

1 CORINTHIANS 12:4-6

There we were, 61 team members—yes, 61!—traipsing into the desert to camp for five days among an unreached Muslim people group. Small groups were dedicated to interaction among women, men, and children. There were sub-teams for storytelling, food prep, worship, and prayer. The logistics for a camp this large were daunting. One person said, "I feel like we just erected a Six Flags amusement park for a week."

Even though we did not know what to expect or whether we would be allowed contact, we planned and prayed together. God blessed, and we found favor with the entire community starting on the first day. Families graciously invited us into their tents. By the second day, there was a steady stream of nomad visitors in our common area enjoying tea, playing games, and engaging in comfortable conversations about life and Jesus.

The team performed a choreographed dance, attending to assigned duties and pitching in wherever they saw a need. It was a great example of the many parts of the body working together for a common goal. God blessed, and people's lives were changed. "For as we have many members in one body, but all the members do not have the same function, so we, being many, are one body in Christ, and individually members of one another" (Romans 12:4-5).

Even in such a Spirit-directed event, there were times I felt overwhelmed with the task. Five days and 61 people is a lot of "different" in one place, and grace really has to kick in. The more grace I give, the more I'll receive from others when I really need it. That's normal. That's life. That's team.

In my experience, the main reason interpersonal challenges arise is lack of communication. It is so easy for tiny remarks or actions to get blown out of proportion and for communication to shut down. My mind can run amok, and before you know it I have assumed the worst about a teammate. Most of the time, the other person does not know he has hurt my feelings or caused confusion. There have been times when I've had to ask for grace and forgiveness from my fellow team members because I was the one who offended. When any of us struggle with relationships, it distracts from our main purpose and drains energy from each other.

Most of us will not go out as Lone Rangers to share the gospel; we will be team players. We will rely on others to fill in our gaps and model the Body of Christ. Living and working as a Live Dead team can be wonderful. We truly can be a powerful army of believers who coordinate endeavors, pray together, and encourage each other through the tough times. May God help us to sacrifice our will daily and offer grace, respect, forgiveness, kindness, and genuine love to each other.

The individuals of every team I have served with have brought more joy to my life than I ever dreamed. No matter the age difference, experience, or background, God takes care of me by providing good counsel, companionship, and someone to share the load. I have learned to appreciate all members of our team and pray God's richest blessing on their lives.

LIVE DEAD CHALLENGE

The Live Dead challenge is first a personal commitment to Jesus and to His concept of team. It often means laying down your will for the will of God and others. Are you currently submitting your gifts, strengths, and personality to God's purpose and the larger purpose of the team you are part of? Look today for the opportunity to celebrate the victory or success of someone else on your ministry team, or in your family, or on your dorm floor, or in your apartment, or in your workplace. Write a note of congratulations expressing how glad you are for this person's effort and achievement.

Read Ephesians 4 and let the words sink deep into your heart.

Enjoy your team. Everyone is a blessing from God.

GRAND COMORIAN

About 300,000 men, women, and children call the volcanic island of N'gazidja home. N'gazidja, or Grand Comore, is an obscure tropical island halfway between the coast of Tanzania and the northwest tip of Madagascar. Grand Comorians have a unique blend of east African and Arab culture with a bit of a French twist. However, don't let the blending of cultures fool you; Grand Comorians are proud of the fact that they are almost 100 percent Muslim.

Farming, fishing, shop keeping, and socializing are the main ways people keep busy. Unemployment is pervasive, so many Grand Comorians pass the day with friends and family. Grand Comorians possess a typical island culture, meaning that most of them dream about the day when they might find the means to leave the island for a better life somewhere else.

Every time it rains, would you pray that God would pour out his love and grace on these islanders. Pray that entire villages would be soaked with the presence and power of the one true King.

Today, my response to working as a team is:

PIONEERING: WHO WILL DARE TO DIE?
BY MARY WALLACE | DJIBOUTI, ETHIOPIA & SOMALIA

In Hargeisa, Somaliland, where my husband and I once lived, the ground is very stony. But sometimes after a rain, tiny brightly colored flowers would appear between the rocks. Though nearly microscopic, each flower was intricate, each beautifully designed. The flowers bloomed in the morning, but by noon all trace that they had once lived was gone.

Isaiah used flowers as a metaphor for the brevity of our lives: "All men are like grass and all their glory as the flowers of the field. The grass withers and the flowers fall …"

My husband and I began our missions career rather naively. We thought all missionaries were pioneers. We had read the biographies of Mary Slessor, Amy Carmichael, Hudson Taylor, David Livingstone, and George Mueller. These men and women were our role models. When God called us to bring the good news to the Somali people, we had been saved for only three years. We hadn't been to Bible college, and for sure we didn't know what apostolic function was. We quit our jobs and sold our house and all our possessions. We bought two one-way tickets to Africa. We held back nothing. We never expected to return; surely we would die in Somalia. After three years in Africa, we got a big shock. My husband became ill and we returned to America, alive. But we were still sold out, and a year and a half later we were back in Somalia.

Though ignorant in the beginning about the face of modern missions, our premise that we would die in Somalia was based in reality. The Somalis have a history of being militantly Muslim. Early on we were mentored by Warren Modriker, an SIM missionary who had spent his life among the Somalis beginning in the 1950s. He sent us a tract he had written for people considering work among Muslims. Most of the tract is now forgotten, but we remember the theme: "Prepare to die."

What we were unprepared for was for our friends and colleagues on the field to die; some young, some talented, and all somehow more valuable to the kingdom than ourselves. We ask ourselves why. Why them, and not us?

Martin, Sheikdon, Christine, Colin, Libaan, Farah—all died for their faith. All died violently. When our dear friend, Martin Utzi, was questioned about the safety of taking his wife and young children to Somaliland, he answered, "If what we are doing is not worth dying for, then it is not worth living for." Only a short time later, as his 3-year-old son looked on, sweet, gentle Martin died from a gunshot to the head. Our friends won't have biographies written about them. Few people know of their sacrifice. Yet, in dying, they show us how to live. Each of us must deliberately be about the work God has called us to do, so that collectively we usher people of every tribe and tongue and nation into the kingdom.

Jim Elliot, martyred by the Waodani tribe of Ecuador, wrote, "He is no fool who gives what he cannot keep, to gain what he cannot lose."

My husband and I have proclaimed and lived the gospel among the Somali people for 25 years. That is not long enough. We are still alive and the Somali people of East Africa are still an unreached people group—and so are the Afar, the Beja, the Boni, the Digo, the peoples of Darfur, the Gosha, the Nubians, the Omani Arabs, the Northern Sudan Arabs, the Yemeni Arabs, the Rashaida, the Shagiyya, the Swahili of Pemba, the Wata.

LIVE DEAD CHALLENGE

Who will go and live among these people groups? Who will dare to die for them? Don't fool yourself into thinking you will die for Jesus overseas, if you will not die to your flesh today. Be on the lookout for some small way to crucify your flesh today.

SOMALI (PUNTLAND)

Somali society is dominated by drug addiction. Their favorite drug is called *khat* or *chat*. It is legal in Africa and comes from the leaves of a bush (Catha edulis). This plant needs lots of water and cool temperatures—growing conditions that are not found in Somalia. The highlands of Ethiopia and Kenya have become the greenhouse for the khat that is consumed in Somalia. The fresh green leaves and new shoots are harvested and then chewed by the user to produce an amphetamine-like high. As soon as the leaves are picked, the active ingredients begin to deteriorate, so the leaves must be bundled quickly and transported at high speed in order to arrive in the hot lowlands of Somalia while they are still fresh.

A large proportion of Somali men use this drug, usually gathering in groups to socialize with fellow users while they chew. Chewing sessions last for hours, and many men chew every day. Money that should be providing food and clothing for the women and children is too often used to buy another bundle of leaves. Puntland is home to most of the Somali pirates, a majority of whom are addicted to khat.

Whenever you see a leafy green bush or someone chewing gum with his mouth open, remember the Somalis and their addiction to chewing khat leaves. Pray that the Lord would deliver them from this drug use.

Today, my response to pioneering is:

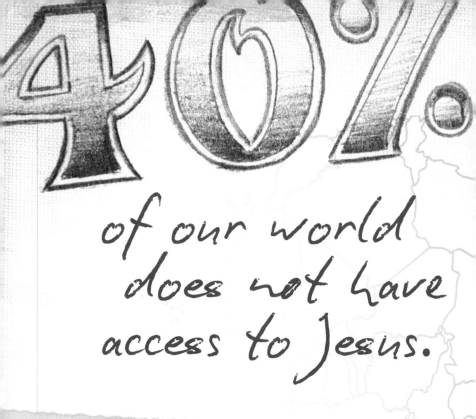

40%

of our world does not have access to Jesus.

TOGETHER, WE ARE RESPONDING TO THIS ONE
PEOPLE GROUP AT A TIME, BY LEARNING THEIR
LANGUAGE, FINDING CULTURALLY RELEVANT
WAYS TO CONNECT, AND GOING TO THEM IN
TEAMS. **YOU CAN BE A PART OF A TEAM TO
REACH THEM BY PRAYING, GIVING, AND GOING.**

FIND OUT HOW AT **WWW.LIVE-DEAD.ORG**

FORGIVENESS: THE EXAMS WILL COME
BY MIKE & KARI NESS | TANZANIA

Bear with each other and forgive whatever grievances you may have against one another. Forgive as the Lord forgave you.

COLOSSIANS 3:13

The story of Jim Elliot and his colleagues who were killed by the Waodani people while trying to reach them with the gospel is known to many of us, but the story of those left behind is not as well known. The wives and loved ones of those men not only continued to pray for the salvation of the Waodani, but some even returned and lived among them so they might hear and see the gospel and come to know Christ. Elliot's widow, Elisabeth, in one of her books, expressed it this way: "The prayers of the widows themselves are for the [Waodani]. We look forward to the day when these savages will join us in Christian praise."

When I hear stories such as this, where people have shown great forgiveness, I ask myself: "Could I forgive in that situation? Would I be able to love the very people who had robbed me of a loved one?" Truth be told, I don't know— and I pray I never have to find out. The real question needing to be asked is: Can I forgive my coworker who spoke something hurtful about me, or my spouse who neglected my feelings and needs? Can I forgive my leader when I am treated unfairly or when there seems to be injustice? We can wonder how we might handle the great offenses of life, even tell ourselves that with God's help we would be forgiving, but what use is it wondering about how we would react to the large offense when we are struggling to forgive our brother for the comparatively small ones?

We can be sure that such offenses will happen in missions. Whether the offender or the offended, the "forgiveness exams" will come; it's in the curriculum. So what do we do when we're hit square in the face with a hurt, a wrong, an offense? We can hold onto that grudge, even nurse it, but we must realize that choice will cost us. We pay a price when we carry around hurt and bitterness. This mark in our heart toward that person constantly nags us; feelings of uneasiness or cynicism toward that person prick at us; their ideas and views are not valued for what they are. All that they say or do is somehow filtered through our unforgiveness. I remember once asking, "What is it going to take for these feelings to go away?" I remember in that very moment the Lord speaking very clearly to me: "Confess. Confess your part in this situation." There was pride and jealousy and hurt under all the layers I had built up over this situation. Buried under all the piles of excuses, as well as the reality of real offenses and hurt, was unforgiveness. My own insecurities did not allow me to see my own mistakes, my own sin. Ouch!

God gives his forgiveness to us at no cost to us other than a confession. Yet it cost Him dearly. When we are called on to forgive, we are called to give it freely. Yet forgiveness has a cost. Forgiveness always costs somebody something. It hurts to give up our hurt, give up our offense. Laying down that "right" to feel this way is not easy. Sometimes we simply have to forgive out of obedience and let our feelings catch up. And even if our feelings never catch up, we are still called to do the right thing, even when it hurts.

Forgiveness has its cost, but its gains are well worth it because it brings freedom. Sometimes the relief is immediate. Sometimes it is a longer process, but freedom will come and we are better people for it. Our words will no longer carry that edge we think others haven't noticed. Our unforgiveness is no longer visible in our jokes, our jabs, and our body language. When there is forgiveness we look differently, feel differently, and respond differently. We can get on with what God wants for us. When we recognize our need to forgive and actually pass the forgiveness exam, we have more emotional energy, we are healthier, and we are free! And that was His plan all along.

LIVE DEAD CHALLENGE

In your time of prayer, ask the Lord to show you any unforgiveness in your heart. Be honest and open and allow Him to sift through your feelings of hurt and wrong to help you get to the heart of the matter—why you really feel the way you do about that person. Confess your part. Maybe there is envy or jealously, your own insecurity that has caused you to feel that way. On a separate piece of paper, list those hurts that person caused you. One by one, give those things to the Lord and confess your forgiveness out loud before the Lord. Sometimes this confession is for you and God alone; other times it must be dealt with between you and the one you struggle with. If there is an obvious rift between you and that person, pray about talking face to face to confess your part in the problem and ask forgiveness and explain how this person has hurt you.

Keep in mind that your feelings may not change overnight. You may have to continue to release that thing to the Lord, whenever those feelings of unforgiveness crop up again. Many times praying for that person, asking God to bless him and prosper him and give him favor will help your heart and attitude change toward him.

UNREACHED PEOPLE GROUP
SOUTH BETSIMISARAKA

The Southern Betsimisaraka people number more than 2 million and are found in the east-central rainforest of Madagascar. These animistic people cultivate rice on the forest hillsides and are responsible for much of the deforestation of Madagascar's once-lush jungles. They have a strong connection with the dead and celebrate yearly those who have passed on. They hold huge feasts and practice numerous rituals to appease and honor their dead ancestors. Wooden poles are erected in the center of each village to honor the ancestors and to show how many cows were offered in sacrifice, the heads of which are impaled on the poles as a testimony.

Many of these villages can be accessed only by small footpaths, and vehicles cannot get through to the vast majority of the Southern Betsimisaraka. Pray for open doors and willing 21st-century circuit-riding preachers to reach these least-reached people. Hiking and motorcycles may be the only ways to reach many of these lost people with the gospel.

Next time you see a motocross bike, think of the Southern Betsimisaraka people and pray for circuit riders with a vision for this lost tribe of Malagasy people.

Today, my response to forgiveness is:

PENTECOST: EMPOWERED BY THE SPIRIT
BY IDA WHITESTONE | SUDAN

When I was 10 years old, I was in Woodworth, Louisiana, for kids camp. Every summer in those altar times, Jesus really met me. That summer was especially memorable for me because I was filled with the Holy Spirit. My parents were chaperones that year, and my daddy was at the altar with me. I remember crying, sobbing for about an hour or longer before I began to pray in the Spirit. I was creating a puddle on the small wooden bench where my father and I knelt. Now that I'm older, I can identify that process as the conviction of the Holy Spirit. John 16:8 shows that conviction is one of the roles of the Holy Spirit.

Living dead is uncomfortable. I am personally not one for confrontation, but with the Holy Spirit we don't have a choice. When we are unpleasing to the Lord, He will let us know it. We don't like to be told that we are wrong, and on top of that we like to make excuses for it. Repentance is an important part of our Christian lives. And on the mission field, it is essential to the health of a team. Living dead isn't about having it all together; it's about confessing our deep need for Jesus to help us get our acts together.

I've seen my pride break under this conviction. When offenses rise, I feel so stubborn and sure that I am not the one who needs to change my attitude; but 10 minutes into my next abiding time I will feel so strongly convicted and know that I need to ask someone's forgiveness. Humility and brokenness are good for the soul, and the reputation.

Jesus has been dropping the phrase "bare reliance" into my heart as I am becoming part of a team to reach an unreached people. There are many things connected to reaching the unreached that no one can really prepare us for; and we need to be reliant on the Holy Spirit to lead us when we don't have a clue what to do.

I believe we can have a tangible connection with Jesus, a "cloud by day, fire by night" leading. We cannot be consistently led or empowered by the Holy Spirit if we are not continually conscious of our need to be refilled with Him. Let us linger when He lingers and let us jump when He moves.

I think our reluctance to rely on the Holy Spirit in a raw way leads to our failure to utilize His power. This is also part of living dead: utilizing His power and giving up ours. Paul warned the Galatians in chapter 4 about returning to the "weak and worthless elementary principles of the world." If we are not living by the Holy Spirit, then that's what we're left with: weak principles of the world.

The principles of the Holy Spirit are power-filled. Are you enslaved to weakness? Backing down or tiptoeing away? Galatians 4:6 tells us that we possess what our Father does.

Living dead also means facing spiritual warfare head on. During language school, I went through a rough season of confusion and doubt. Islam was beginning to invade my mind. One day in prayer, I realized that I had this sudden misconception that God had manipulated me into this life, that He had a hidden agenda and was somehow not truthful in how He approached me to follow Him this way. I was so discouraged and I wanted out. Something told me this wasn't right, but I was so confused in my heart about it.

I was crying out to the Lord for clarity of mind, and suddenly I started to scream out words that I didn't plan on. I started saying: "That is not my God! Jesus is pure! There is no crooked way in Him! His heart is pure! His heart is for me! There is no evil in His nature!" These simple truths were fixed again in my heart and mind. The Holy Spirit fought for me in this time of warfare. There are many more times of spiritual warfare ahead of us, and He is ready to fight. We need Him to wash away lies and do what we simply do not have the power in ourselves to do, because many times, we can't even see our enemy.

LIVE DEAD CHALLENGE

If you have been raised without hearing much emphasis on the Holy Spirit or the baptism in the Spirit and are afraid of it or don't know how to feel about it, spend time releasing any of that fear to the Lord. Fear and resistance usually come because of a lack of knowledge or understanding. Read Acts 1 through 4 and ask Jesus to fill you with His Spirit. Get ready for conviction, power, boldness, comfort, and guidance to enter your life in a new way.

Think of anyone who has offended you recently and ask the Holy Spirit where you need to repent. Ask this person for forgiveness today.

Begin praying in the Spirit for 10 minutes each morning. Pray in the Spirit in the "lull" moments in your day and while driving. Turn off your radio and let the Holy Spirit fill your car as you commune with Him.

SOMALI

When two Somali people meet for the first time, they begin reciting their genealogy backward until they find a common ancestor. A traditional Somali child will be required to learn his or her father's ancestry back 800 years, and learning the mother's lineage can also come in handy. The Somali are the largest people group on the Horn of Africa. Many of the 2.4 million Somalis living in Kenya, who are 99.9 percent Muslim, have lived here for generations while others have migrated because of the unrest and political instability of Somalia.

Whenever you meet someone for the first time, pray for the Somali of Kenya. The key to reaching the Horn of Africa is the Somali people.

Today, my response to the Holy Spirit is:

HOW FEW THERE ARE WHO DIE SO HARD

"Most assuredly I say to you, unless a grain of wheat falls into the ground and dies, it remains alone, but if it dies it produces much fruit."

JOHN 12:24

The Live Dead challenge has a specific goal—the raising up of missionaries who will join teams planting churches among unreached peoples. In order to reach these peoples with the gospel of Jesus Christ, we are going to have to live a certain way. We must live dead.

Living dead is not a morbid call to self-flagellation. Living dead is a call to life, and life abundant. Living dead is a call to radical love for Jesus and sacrificial love for the world. Living dead is a call to announce the life of God among the perishing. Living dead is an admission that in order to reach the lost, there is much of our flesh that must die so the life of God might be manifest in our mortal bodies. We die that Christ lives in us. We die that others may live.

Samuel Zwemer, known as "the Apostle to Islam," quotes Charles Spurgeon in his book, *The Glory of the Impossible:* " 'All power is given unto Me. ... Lo I am with you always.' You have a factor here that is absolutely infinite, and what does it matter what other factors may be. 'I will do as much as I can,' says one. *Any fool can do that.* He that believes in Christ does what he cannot do, attempts the impossible, and performs it."

Zwemer goes on to say: "Frequent setbacks and apparent failure never disheartened the real pioneer. Occasional martyrdoms are only a fresh incentive. Opposition is stimulus to greater activity. Great victory has never been possible without great sacrifice. ... War always means blood and treasure. Our only concern should be to keep the fight aggressive and to win victory regardless of cost or sacrifice. The unoccupied fields of the world must have their Calvary, before they can have their Pentecost."

He continues: "It was the bigness of the task and its difficulty that thrilled the early church. Its impossibility was its glory, its worldwide character, its grandeur. The same is true today. There are hundreds ... who expect to spend life practicing law or in some trade for a livelihood. … They are making a living; they might be making a life."

The Live Dead challenge is an invitation to make a life. Make a life that counts for eternity. Under the guidance and power of the Holy Spirit, attempt the impossible and for the glory of Christ live and die among an unreached people of earth. Die to your self that Jesus might live through you, and extend His ineffable love to those who have never heard.

We refuse to pretend that this is easy practically, relationally, or spiritually. We refuse to claim that any missionary currently working among the unreached has arrived. We are all in the messy process of dying, and it is as difficult to experience as it is to observe. Adoniram Judson lived and died for Burma (present-day Myanmar), and three of his wives and six of his children perished in the effort. He was tortured, he was abused, he suffered. He left behind him the first translation of the Bible, the first dictionary, and the first believers who would grow into thousands of churches with millions of followers of Jesus. On his deathbed in great agony he said, "How few there are who die so hard."

Will you be one of those few?

William Whiting Borden was a graduate of Yale and Princeton. He was saved under the ministry of D. L. Moody and called to be a missionary to China. Borden came from a wealthy family, and he renounced all his inherited fortune, writing "No Reserve" in his Bible when he did so. His father tried to convince him to return to the family wealth and business, but he refused again, and wrote in his Bible, "No Retreat." On the way to China he contracted spinal meningitis in Cairo. Just before he died, he scrawled one more declaration: "No Regrets."

No reserve. No retreat. No regrets.

To live dead means to live with no reserve. Nothing left, nothing saved, all used up for the gospel. To live dead means no retreat. Following Jesus though none go with us, none approve, and none understand. To live dead means no regrets, even if—as with Borden—we accomplish nothing but obedience.

We must in the same spirit of Judson, Borden, the Apostles, and most importantly Jesus, live and die for the unreached. We must send missionaries to the Somalias of the world. We must all live dead, senders and goers alike. For everyone that dies—many will live. For everyone that is killed—we will send a dozen more. We will live and die without reserve, without retreat, without regrets.

Bishop Phillips Brooks challenges us all:

> *Do not pray for easy lives; pray to be stronger men*
> *Do not pray for tasks equal to your powers*
> *Pray for powers equal to your tasks*
> *Then the doing of your work shall be no miracle*
> *But you shall be a miracle.*

If you are willing to live dead with us, to join a church-planting team that is working among unreached peoples, please contact us at www.Live-Dead.org.

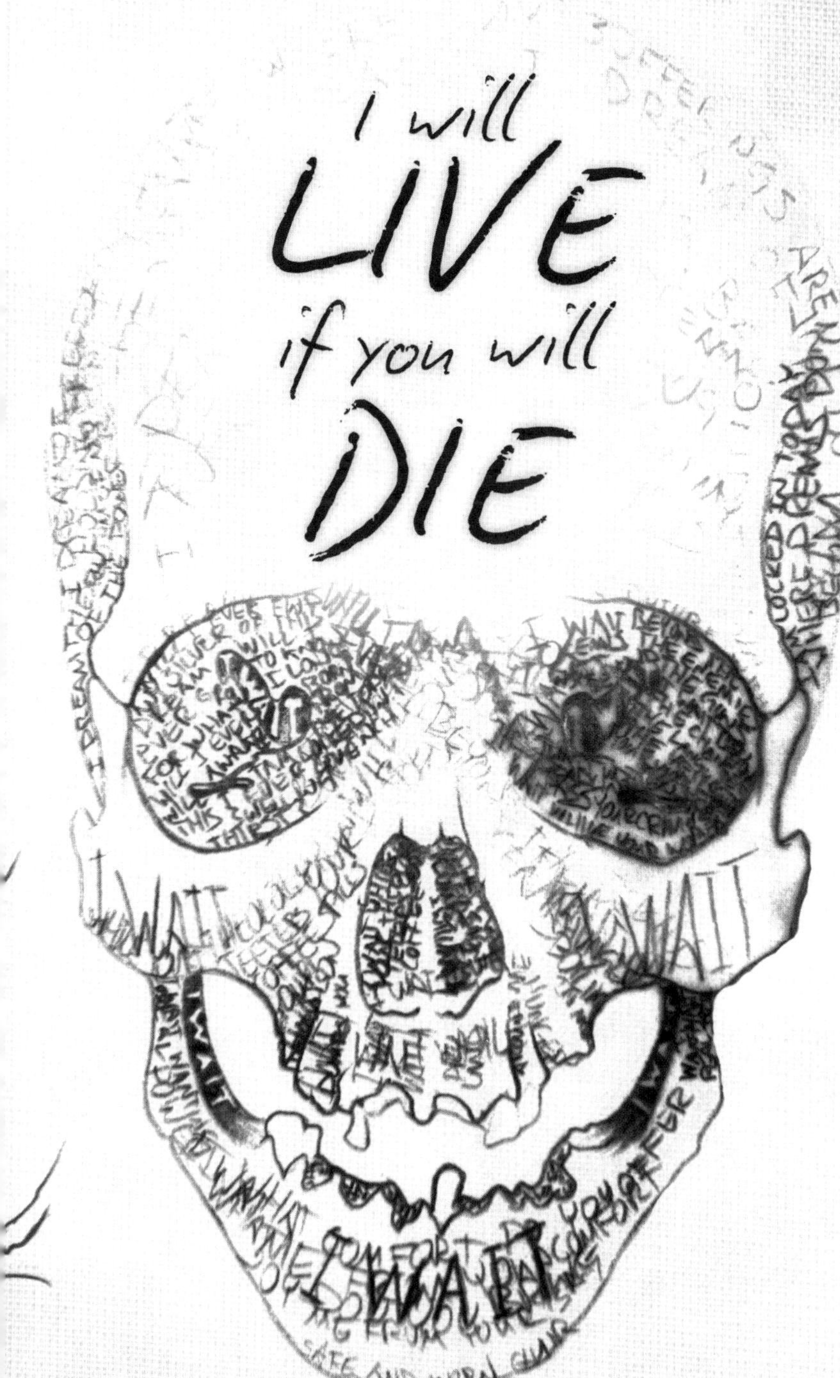
I will
LIVE
if you will
DIE
I WAIT

ABOUT THE COLLABORATORS

DICK BROGDEN, LIVE DEAD ARAB WORLD

Dick and Jennifer Brogden have been treasuring Jesus among Muslims in Mauritania (1992), Kenya (1993-95), Sudan (1995-2011), and North Africa (2011-present). Their two sons, Luke and Zack, were born in Sudan and consider themselves Africans. The Brogdens love Jesus with all their broken hearts and long that every ancient gate may be lifted up that Jesus, strong and mighty, King of Glory, may come in. They believe that God is best glorified in mission when His people work in multinational teams to reach the unreached and to plant the church where Christ has not been named.

GREG BEGGS, AFRICA REGIONAL DIRECTOR

Greg and Danna Beggs started their missionary service in 1987 in Tanga, Tanzania. They worked with the Tanzanian AG in youth ministries and church planting, and started an extension Bible school program for church planters. In 2000, they moved to Kenya. Since then, they have had the honor of serving the missionaries and national churches of the 17 countries of East Africa and the Indian Ocean Basin.

SCOTT HANSON, STRATEGIC LEADER
UNREACHED PEOPLE GROUPS

Scott and Karen Hanson are dedicated to seeing Christ taken to places where He is unknown and unavailable. They both grew up in Africa, where they were raised by missionary parents who were passionate about seeing the gospel taken to remote areas. As missionaries since 1994, Scott and Karen have devoted their lives to raising up African missionaries to take the gospel to people and places where Christ is not known and the church is not established. They have two daughters, Megan and Makenzie, who love Africa as their home.

STEVE PENNINGTON, EAST AFRICA AREA DIRECTOR

Steve and Trina have served East Africa for nearly 20 years. They began their ministry in 1994 in Nairobi, Kenya, serving an unreached people group that had occupied their hearts for many years. From 1997 to 2007, they lived in Addis Ababa, Ethiopia, and worked with the Ethiopia Assemblies of God and the Addis Ababa Bible College. They returned to Nairobi in 2007 to serve the Kenya Assemblies of God at the East Africa School of Theology and in other roles. The privilege of serving with Live Dead answers a lifelong yearning to see Christ worshipped where His name is not now known. The Lord has given them Josiah, Priscilla, and Micah—MKs who love Jesus and consider themselves East African.

THE LIVE DEAD WRITERS

The *Live Dead Journal* contributors are missionaries who live and serve among the world's least-reached peoples. Young and old, male and female, they share a common passion to see the church planted where it does not exist. They are not heroes; they are simply trying to be obedient, struggling to live dead, that Jesus might be glorified.

CHARITY REEB, CREATIVE DIRECTOR

Charity Reeb is a brand and marketing strategist with a heart to inspire people to go out and be Jesus' hands and feet to the unreached world. She is passionate about using the arts to communicate stories in a relevant way. Charity and her husband, Jeff, live in Springfield, Missouri, and travel to some of the world's most remote and lost locations to meet people, work with missionaries, and tell stories through campaigns such as Live Dead.

AUSTIN EVANS, ARTIST

After spending most of his life traveling the United States, Austin Evans lives in Springfield, Missouri, where he raises his daughter and owns and operates Transformation Gallery & Tattoo. Although he has always been deeply involved in art, it was not until recently that he realized God's call on his life, to spread the love of Christ through his artwork. He spends his free time painting and raising his daughter with the knowledge of the love, power, and sacrifice of Christ.

GABE TENNESON, ARTIST

Despite a belief in God, Gabe Tenneson lacked a personal relationship with Him for the first 20 years of his life. He sank deeper and deeper into the darkness of the world until he found himself on the proverbial brink. At that point, he chose to die to himself and live dead for his Father. God has since harnessed Gabe's artistic talent into a call to reach the tattooing community. He is an owner of Transformation Gallery & Tattoo.

JOSH TENNESON, ARTIST

Josh Tenneson is passionate about the arts and music. He is employed by Transformation Gallery & Tattoo, which is dedicated to the creation and advancement of fine art. But he says all of his existence is nothing without his one true ardor: "God. My Father. My Keeper. And the Love of my life. He alone has blessed me with true life, and He alone has privileged me with my talents and passions."

MIKE MURRAY, EDITOR

Mike and Nikki Murray are missionaries to the university students of the post-Soviet, Muslim nations of Central Eurasia. They are dedicated to proclaiming the gospel and making disciples among the unreached. Prior to their appointment with AGWM in 2004, Mike worked for 10 years as a newspaper reporter and magazine editor. They have three children: Anna, Evan, and Colin.

LUCENT DIGITAL, GRAPHIC DESIGN

Designers Kelsey Baldwin and Jason Nill at Lucent Digital brought the Live Dead stories and artwork together, bringing this journal to life. Lucent Digital is a design studio in Springfield, Missouri. Founded in 2003 by missionary kids, their team has a passion for helping those who do good look good. In addition to book design, Lucent Digital specializes in brand identity design, websites, and digital marketing.

SPECIAL THANKS

Special thanks to Michael Buesking for the "Survivor" painting on page 69.

LIVE | DEAD

Live Dead The Journey ▶

◀ *Live Dead The Story*

Live Dead Joy ▶

◀ *The Live Dead Journal:*
Her Heart Speaks

Live Dead India:
The Common Table ▶

Live Dead Life ▶

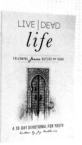

◀ This Gospel

Leading Muslims to Jesus ▶

◀ Live Dead Together

Live Dead Journal Spanish ▶

Check out the full line of Live Dead devotionals
in the Live Dead online store at *livedead.org*.

join the movement

The Live Dead Journal has been a catalyst for those God is calling to the unreached. If you are sensing God's leading to missions, we want to talk to you and answer any questions you may have. Email us at *advocacy@livedead.org*.

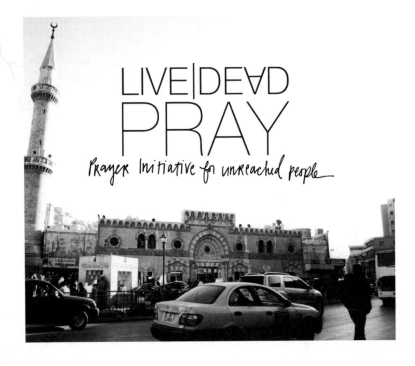

LIVE|DEAD PRAY

Prayer Initiative for unreached people

Live Dead Pray aims prayerful hearts of believers at the unreached people groups throughout the world.
Sign up today at *livedead.org/pray* and we will provide you with the resources to start a Live Dead Pray Band.